What People Are Saying about
The Settlement Game

"This is a life-changing book that will help you protect and preserve your family relationships as you go through the inevitable process of dividing up all the personal property of an estate. All of us—and our children—will face this issue some day. This book will tell you how to do this and remain friends."

"It seems obvious to me that the author's plan is worthy of dissemination in book form and that the book will be widely used by all who are faced with the important task of settling the problems, which are necessarily a part of the orderly transfer of property."

"Thank you for helping us with the settlement of Mom's estate using the information in your book, *The Settlement Game*. I recommend this to anyone who cares about protecting healthy, loving relationships . . . this could be responsible for transforming an otherwise negative and difficult process into a joyful and pleasant relationship builder.

"Without hesitation, I recommend this publication to anyone who is faced with the responsibility of dividing the material assets of a parent. It is a practical and common-sense approach to making a very difficult task much easier."

"In *The Settlement Game*, Angie Epting Morris makes a vital contribution to America's families. So many hurts happen in the aftermath of grief that damaging conflict over possessions should be avoided. This book is a down to earth conversation based on experience as well as observation about how to prepare for working constructively through the decisions to be made about division of possessions. Preparing beforehand avoids regretting afterwards."

—JIMMY R. ALLEN, JR
Past President of Southern Baptist Convention,
Big Canoe, Georgia

"None of us would prefer to deal with estate planning and settlement, but it is an inevitable fact of life, and it is best to be prepared. Angie Morris has put together a very interesting plan to avoid pain and hurt feelings when dealing with sensitive estate settlements. *The Settlement Game* offers an opportunity to bring about effective communication and resourceful planning, making a difficult time in life easier to manage."

—LORAN SMITH
Contributing Writer and President Georgia Bulldog Club,
Athens, Georgia

"Angie Epting Morris has written a powerful book. *The Settlement Game* provides a common sense solution to a proven problem. I commend Angie for sharing her experience and wisdom with the world. Relationships are precious."

—MARGARET S. ROSS, President
Kamaron Institute, Peachtree City, Georgia

"Thank you so much for sharing *The Settlement Game* with us. We had a very special time of settling everything up. It was a great way to remember fun times and share "remember when" stories as we were playing the game. Everyone was pleased with the division, and there were no hurt feelings anywhere. This is something I would recommend to every family!"

—CATHY MCMILLAN
McMillan & Associates, Birmingham, Alabama

The
Settlement
Game

How to Settle an Estate
Peacefully and Fairly

Angie Epting Morris

Foreword by Griffin B. Bell

Voyages Press, Inc.
BIG CANOE, GEORGIA

First printing 2006

ISBN-13: 978-0-9769934-2-1   LCCN: 2005928362
ISBN-10: 0-9769934-2-2

ATTENTION CORPORATIONS, LAW FIRMS,
ESTATE AND FINANCIAL PLANNERS, FUNERAL HOMES,
AND PROFESSIONAL ORGANIZATIONS

877-835-8449; www.thesettlementgame.com.

Our parents were Eugene Albert Epting and Frances Thomas Epting. They lived in Athens, Georgia, for their 54 years of marriage (1939–1993). He was a native of Athens, and she was originally from Ennis, Texas.

Dedication

This book is dedicated to our "Daddy," in loving memory and with gratitude for his positive example. He taught us how to live and how to love. He was the most honest and ethical and also the most "peaceful and fair" man I have ever known. His life was a living example of integrity, honor, and love. He would be proud to know that all four of his children did indeed listen to his words of wisdom through all of those years. It is my greatest hope that this book will serve as a fitting tribute to him. And to our Mother, who was his devoted wife and his greatest admirer.

Also, in loving memory of our firstborn son, Hodges Carter Morris, Jr. (30 May 1975). Although he did not survive birth, his memory has made a difference in our lives.

God works in wondrous ways. On the morning when my husband and my doctor stood by my side to tell me of my son's birth and that he did not survive, I immediately felt a presence of peace that flooded over me and comforted me and kept me strong. It truly was a "peace that passeth all understanding." It has remained with me from that day forward, stronger at times than others, but nonetheless, ever present. Perhaps it is simply the fact that once I recognized God's necessary presence in my life, I have always remained aware that He was there to help.

In the weeks and months that followed, the lessons of life that I learned as a result of this heartache have impacted my life in ways I could never fully explain. Some of the truths that came from that experience were offered as words of comfort from friends and family. Other truths have been realized in looking back at my life and seeing God's hand in it all. Sometimes the true meaning of these sayings did not become evident until years later. Following are those most meaningful to me.

Be thankful for your troubles, for they are the tools by which God fashions you for greater things.

In every adversity lies a seed of equal or better benefit.

God is in His heaven; All is right in the world.

Coincidence is God's way of working anonymously.

Some of these quotes may seem trite and overworked or even out of place in a book of this sort. I offer them here because they are truths that have made it possible for me to write this book. More importantly, by suggesting them, I hope they will help to show there is always something good that can come from anything bad that happens.

I should add that a few years after losing our firstborn, we were blessed with two wonderful sons, Hunter (b. 1978) and Taylor (b. 1980). They have been told since they were born that we believe they are truly gifts to us from God. They are special, and they are great friends with us and with each other. This book is therefore also dedicated to Hunter and Taylor. It is my earnest prayer they will use it to protect and preserve their special relationship as brothers in the eventual settlement of our personal estate, be it large or small.

I believe God is available to everyone on earth in a manner as described above. The important thing we must do is recognize that this powerful resource is available to us, if we will only seek His help and guidance. I also believe that God's answers and actions don't always match what we had in mind. However, He always provides in the way and timing that is best—if we can just trust Him to do so.

Whether experiencing a devastating loss of a parent or other loved one, or simply trying to prevent problems for the future, God is always with you and available to help you. All you have to do is ask Him and allow him to work in His way and His time. I believe in prayer. It has sustained me through all the trials of life. And it is my prayer that this book will serve you in many ways to help protect and preserve your family relationships. And even if you feel your situation is beyond hope, I pray this book (with God's help) will serve to help repair the damaged relationships.

Table of Contents

Foreword
by Griffin B. Bell

This useful volume by Angie Epting Morris will help readers to divide the family property of deceased parents in a fair and peaceful manner.

It is not unusual in our time for the children of a family to live away from the home of the parents and in several places. The author and her siblings all lived far away from the home of their parents in Athens, Georgia. None expected to return there. Their ancestral home with all of its furnishings had to be divided among four children or sold, and the house had to be prepared for sale.

How to accomplish these things in good spirit and without rancor or even dissatisfaction was the objective of the children. The author describes the plan used in achieving this objective. Their father, a prominent lawyer of much experience, could not have done a better job himself. Their effort, including the result, reflects great credit on the father, whom they were hoping to emulate.

The method used in the Epting estate is a common-sense approach, and it can easily be adapted to any situation wherein property is to be divided among several heirs. Each heir gets his or her choice, and what is left is sold with the funds to be divided equally. The appraisal, which is needed in any estate disposition, is the key to the division; it is the first of several steps in the process.

It seems obvious to me that the author's plan is worthy of dissemination in book form and that the book will be widely used by all who are faced with the important task of settling the problems, which are necessarily a part of the orderly transfer of property.

—Griffin B. Bell

Judge Griffin B. Bell is a senior counsel in the law firm of King and Spalding, LLP, with offices in Atlanta, Houston, London, New York, and Washington, DC. Judge Bell served as the 72nd Attorney General of the United States from January 1977 until August 1979, in the administration of President Jimmy E. Carter. See complete biographical information about Judge Bell on page 115.

Introduction and Overview

This book provides a step-by-step guide for dividing up the material things of an estate in a peaceful manner. It aims to provide a method by which family relationships can be protected, preserved, and even improved. The plan is designed to help people avoid conflict and to teach them how to have family fun instead of a family feud.

I believe in family relationships. They are special and unique and should be among our most precious possessions. However, throughout my life, I have heard countless horror stories about how families have been torn apart by fights that are rooted in hard feelings after dividing up a family estate. And I am not necessarily talking about the type of estates that are large and complicated. It doesn't necessarily take a lot of stuff to make up an "estate." Basically, whatever is left to be divided after the death of a family member qualifies as "an estate."

Most wills make some specific requests about larger things, but the furniture and household goods usually get lumped together at the end of the will with a sentence like: "...and all other property to be divided equally among my heirs." There's just one problem: *How* do you divide all of that stuff equally? Hardly anyone really seems to know a proven method to recommend.

Shortly after our parents died in 1993, we discovered that we were not sure about how to divide up all the household things. When we asked our attorney, who was also a close family friend, he could only suggest that we "do something like draw straws—but most importantly," he said "…remain friends." And that was the problem! For various reasons, we all worried that we would end up with hurt feelings or resentment for one another, and we really didn't know what specifically to do. We did already know the importance of "remaining friends," but we needed to find a way to divide things evenly so that we would all walk away happy when the process was complete.

The method we developed, which we now call *The Settlement Game*, is thoroughly documented in this book. Although no two families will have the exact same situation, this process can easily be adapted to fit almost any set of circumstances. Since our parents' deaths, we have told many people about *The Settlement Game*. Finally, I began to write it out for others to use. As the stories trickled back about how helpful the process had been, I realized this was something that could benefit countless numbers of people. It is a fact that death is inevitable, so all of us will face this difficult time of life. Most people will have to deal first with the deaths of their parents and then will have to prepare for their own passing and the futures of their children. Therefore, this book applies to just about everyone.

Disclaimer

Although this method of dividing up an estate should help greatly in preventing conflict and protecting relationships, it is certainly not guaranteed to do so. In some cases, it may only help to improve situations that have been negative for years. If there have been relationship problems brewing within a family for years, this process might even create an environment in which problems "rise to the surface." Such an occurrence could prove to be helpful in the long run, however, if those problems are ultimately solved or at least addressed by the heirs.

The author makes no claim that this is a "foolproof" process. However, *The Settlement Game* does offer some beneficial recommendations that have proven helpful in many estate divisions to date. The methods presented here have been in use since 1993. Most of the stories used to illustrate the methods were actually related to the author personally by a family member involved in an estate settlement. All names have been changed, however, and any similarities between a story about persons with fictional names and events concerning real persons with those same names is purely coincidental.

Acknowledgments

With loving and sincere thanks to:

First, my three siblings who were all part of the development of this process:

Jean Epting Mosshart—For being our organizer and excellent record keeper. Your good work and diligence made all of this possible. Through the process, you became a great friend. Also, thanks to Roger for his patience, kindness, assistance, and his truck.

Al Epting—For putting up with your three sisters all of your life. Also, for your quiet calm in times of turmoil and for reminding us by your actions of Daddy's wit and wisdom throughout the process.

Fae Epting Davidson—For suggesting the final name of the book and for assistance with organization of content. Also, for staying connected and faithful to us from so far away. Thanks to Trapper, as well, for his patience and kindness.

Then, also, to:

Carter Morris, my husband—For inspiring me to publish this finally, by showing your confidence in me when you asked me to share this book with your family for use in settling your Mom's estate. I am proud and honored to be your wife and to be sharing life's journey with you. Your tough love gives me a safe place to land. Thanks for being loyal and strong and a man of great character.

Hunter Morris and Taylor Morris, my sons—For giving me purpose and inspiration to finish this so that *The Settlement Game* can be passed on to you for use in settling our estate one day. Thanks for embracing our values and for making us proud. You are both special gifts to us from God.

Mary Carter Morris—For being my friend first, then my mother-in-law. Her uplifting encouragement and understanding have always been treasured. Her kind generosity has made the publication of this book possible.

Lee Erwin Epting—For teaching me how to dream big and reach for the stars. Your zest for life is infectious. Thanks for sharing so much of life with me. As our cousin, you are a part of this legacy. Thanks for representing the Epting name so honorably.

Margaret Epting Medlock—For continuing to be an inspiration to us and for joining us in recalling happy memories with stories about our heritage. Also, for your unending love. Your attitude is always refreshing.

Grace and Kenneth Waters—For your unconditional love and friendship, not only with our parents throughout the years, but also with us as well.

Billy and Peggy Florence—For seeing the potential in this subject and for originally suggesting that I set it down in book form. Also, for being the first outside of our immediate family to use this method to settle an estate. Thanks, as well, for your love and support and belief in me always.

Jerry and Linda Hardin—For continuing to be our friends and for standing by us and with us through the trials of life. Your friendship is ever-faithful and unconditional, which is priceless.

Craig and Linnie Baynham—For being special friends and for being a part of my Team. You always lift me up and encourage me, for which I am grateful. Sharing life's experiences with you is both fun and inspiring.

Dot Parrish—Your publishing experiences have been an inspiration to me. Thanks for your enthusiasm and for encouraging me to tackle this topic in the beginning phase of this project. Also, thanks for sharing your promotional ideas.

Will Caskey—For patiently educating me on matters related to estate planning, wills, and other financial concerns and for encouraging me along the way. Both your advice and friendship are cherished.

John Brooks—Thanks for sharing my vision about this book and what it can be. Your expertise has been invaluable on cover design and website development. Also, your attitude has added to the enjoyment of this experience. And thanks for helping to prove my belief that "Coincidence is God's way of working anonymously."

And to all the friends, relatives, and acquaintances who have encouraged me and voiced approval about this topic. Your uplifting attitudes have inspired me to finish this project. Thank you, one and all.

1

How to Use This Book

You Will Still Need a Family Attorney

The Settlement Game is not intended to be used as a replacement for the important and necessary legal services of an attorney. In fact, this book is written in a manner that may prove most beneficial if used by attorneys to suggest a method of division to clients faced with the task of settling an estate. There are many important *legal* matters of an estate settlement that are *not* covered in this book. *The Settlement Game* is intended to serve only as a guide for making a fair and even distribution of the material and monetary possessions of an estate that have not been specifically designated in a will.

Who Should Read This Book
Everyone Involved in the Settlement!

I recommend that everyone involved in the settlement of an estate should read through this entire book from cover to cover before any attempt is made to apply its principles to an individual situation. There are many little parts and pieces to the process. Without a thorough understanding of the overall concept of *The Settlement Game*, it could prove to be slightly confusing. Every aspect of the process has been presented in great detail. By the end of the book, you should be able to see the overall method and be able to apply it. The book can be read fairly quickly, and doing so will help make the complete process easier for everyone involved. Since the method presented here is a very adaptable process, this book is intended as a basic guideline in assisting you in designing your own "Settlement Game."

How Your Heirs Will Settle Your Estate
What Can Go Wrong...A Word of Caution!

For obvious reasons, this is often a sensitive subject to discuss. However, I hope to suggest some things for you to think about if you are in the situation of planning how you intend for your heirs to settle your estate. Using personal examples from stories told to me from others may best illustrate these points.

Because I have given a rough version of this plan to so many people over the last few years, I have heard many stories from them about relatives or acquaintances of theirs who have had negative experiences while dividing an estate. Although the main intent of this book is to provide suggestions of a positive nature in order to help prevent problems, it seems appropriate to provide some examples of things that can go wrong in order to illustrate how this book can help you avoid them. I have chosen four examples, but based on the number of stories I have heard over the years, it is probably safe to say that everyone reading this book could relate at least one tragic story of relationships damaged by the situations surrounding the division of furniture and other personal items that belonged to a deceased parent. I have also discovered that the majority of those who have related such stories to me have started off by saying they never would have believed anything like this could have happened in *their* family. That should serve as a word of caution.

The old adage "an ounce of prevention is worth a pound of cure" comes to mind here. Unfortunately, the turmoil often produced during this process of trying to settle an estate usually leaves a permanent scar on the family. Resentments may never be overcome, or if they are, only after many years of strained relationships within a family. I am willing to bet that at least one of the following examples will remind you of a similar story you have either heard or experienced personally.

Example 1: After hearing countless stories, it finally occurred to me that one of the biggest problems that arises in the process of settling an estate seems to be caused by the parents themselves, who really had intended to try to prevent problems. One of the things I've often heard is how a parent would attempt to prevent heirs from fighting over an estate by predetermining specifically "who gets what" or by going ahead and giving things away in advance. Although the intent here is honorable and seems appropriate, these approaches are often a major source of conflict later. Here's how it might go:

Let's say Mrs. Thomas has four daughters: Sally, Jane, Beth, and Ann. Twenty years after the girls have left home and married, Mama decides to take care of estate matters and begins to designate certain items to go to her individual daughters, with the well-meaning purpose of preventing arguments among them later. She designates an antique bed in the guest room for Sally and a special dresser of equal value for Jane (and so forth).

After Mrs. Thomas has passed away, the girls come together to settle the estate and divide up the furniture and household goods, etc. At some point in the process, Jane discovers that her mother has given "her" bed to Sally. Jane loved that bed, and it was in her room all through the years while she was growing up. She is sure this must be a mistake. Sally is delighted, because she loves the bed too and thinks it will be perfect for her daughter's room. Since her daughter is the only "granddaughter," Sally is certain that is why Mama gave it to her...

Well, you know the rest of the story. It happens over and over, innocently, but feelings get hurt and resentments last a long time—often forever.

The problem was, Mama didn't really remember that the bed had been in Jane's room in earlier years. The girls had been away from home for more than twenty years, and she had turned that room into the guest room. She had come to think of that bed as just "the bed in the guest room." In this manner, Mama may actually have caused conflict instead of prevented it.

Example 2: Another situation that I hear often relates to parents giving things away to grandchildren or others, unmindful of the ramifications. Of course there are going to be small things of that sort that are a natural part of life, but what I am referring to is the attempt to clean out the house by giving away stuff without considering all of the children or heirs. This most often happens when some of the heirs live in the same town, but others live far away. This story is an example of what often happens when a parent is still living and attempts to predetermine the destiny of her "things"—in this story, jewelry. Once again, the intent is wonderful—but consider the dynamics of the relationships after the settlement is over:

One Christmas, after the dinner dishes have been cleared from the table, Mrs. Taylor spreads out all of her "valuable" jewelry on the dining room table. Since all of her children and their spouses and all of the grandchildren are present, this seems like a perfect time to take care of designating who gets what of her jewelry, so that when she dies, there will be no arguments over these decisions.

She calls all of the female members of the family into the dining room and states her intent. Each one is to choose an item from the collection. She designates the order for the selection: oldest daughter first, then her son's wife since he was the second child, then her younger daughter, then the oldest granddaughter, etc. She knows the men are not interested in the jewelry, so in this category they are not considered. As the daughters make their selections, Mrs. Taylor writes it all down and then tells them that after she is gone, they will immediately receive the item they have chosen.

As innocent and well planned as this may seem, the problems with such a method could be many. First of all, the male members of the family are left out completely, except for the wife of the son—who will now become resented by the two daughters. Then there is the problem of value. Some may know the value of items, but others may not, so there would probably be a great difference in value received, especially by the younger granddaughters. Overall, rather than preventing problems, Mrs. Taylor's innocent method may have actually created problems that will surface later.

(Chapter 4 discusses the importance of having an appraisal done, as it will determine the value of items being divided. The importance of this information is explained further in this chapter. In Chapter 7—Keeping Score, the importance of this step will be even more clearly illustrated.)

How an Estate Plan Differs from a Will

Perhaps this is a good place to explain what an estate plan means and how it differs from a will. With the excellent assistance of Mr. Will Caskey of Merrill Lynch, our financial and estate planning advisor and our friend, here is a description of this important difference. Some of this information was also taken from the website of the NAEPC (National Association of Estate Planners & Councils), www.NAEPC.org.

An estate plan is the desire and intent of how all assets and property will be transferred from one person (or couple) to the next person (or generation.) A will can be one component of an estate plan, but it alone cannot effectively complete the estate plan. A will names whom you want to handle your final affairs and whom you want to receive your assets after you die. However, most people don't know that a will only controls the assets that are titled in your name. It does not control assets that are titled in joint ownership and go to your spouse or another joint owner when you die. It does not control assets with beneficiary designations like your retirement accounts, such as IRA, Roth IRA, Annuities, 401(k), 403(b), and Profit Sharing plans, and life insurance policies. A will also does not go into effect until one is deceased. A properly executed Power of Attorney is needed for the time between when one is no longer able to handle one's own affairs and death.

Once death occurs, those assets that can be controlled by the will must go through a court-controlled process called "probate." Probate is the legal process through which the court system makes sure that after you die your will is valid, your debts are paid, and your assets are distributed according to your will. Probate costs vary from state to state depending upon where assets are owned. At the very minimum, it is a time-consuming process as the executor(trix) makes their way through the process. If real property is owned in more than one location, the will must be probated in each of the counties or states where property is owned. Even for modest estates, one can expect the process to take from one to three years. Oftentimes a will is quite sufficient to handle all the affairs of one's estate. However, it is important that each will be specifically designed and properly executed for individuals with their specific situations and circumstances in mind.

Another component or tool for estate planning is the use of titling assets in joint ownership. Most married people title assets together using a title called "joint tenants with right of survivorship" (commonly abbreviated JTWROS). This leaves the entire balance of the assets to the surviving joint owner. It is a very simple and effective tool that easily handles homes, automobiles, and checking accounts. It is important to note that this designation supersedes the will.

Gifting assets away to another party while one is still alive is another effective technique in an overall estate plan. There are important tax considerations surrounding gifting that must be discussed with a competent tax advisor. One can only give away assets up to a certain value (currently $11,000 per person, per year) without the donor incurring a gift tax. Also, the asset is given with the original cost basis and if sold by the recipient can incur capital gains tax to the recipient if the asset is highly appreciated in value from the original purchase. On the benefit side, if the asset is given to a charitable organization, it may result in a tax deduction. Perhaps the greatest benefit to gifting while one is alive is to see the recipient enjoy the gift and benefit from it at an earlier age.

A Revocable Living Trust is another alternative or addition to a will in a more comprehensive estate plan. This trust is its own entity like a person or a corporation. It is called a Revocable Living Trust because it is established while one is living and can be changed or "revoked" by the donor at any time. When it is established, one designates himself or herself as the "trustee" of the trust. All assets that one wants to be controlled by the trust are then placed into the trust by a transfer of title. The trust will also designate who the successor trustees are, much as a corporation has a chain of command or succession. The trust can have an open-ended life with the successor trustees. Since the assets are owned by the trust, probate is avoided because the assets never change hands again unless the final instructions of the trust are to distribute them to a named beneficiary. This type of trust also avoids the need for a Power of Attorney in the event one no longer can (or desires) to handle one's own affairs. The successor trustee simply steps up and begins to control the named assets.

Another decision in estate planning is to do nothing. If one dies with no valid will in place, one is deemed to have died "intestate." As mentioned before, beneficiary designations will be honored, but the laws of the state in which one owns property or assets will control all probate assets. This lack of control may cause assets to be distributed in a manner that is less than desirable. Some states, for example, divide assets equally among surviving children and the surviving spouse.

The important thing to do is to have financial, tax, and legal professionals work together to help you create an estate plan. In many instances, a complete estate plan includes all of the items discussed above. They will work together to achieve the goal of an effective estate plan. Attention to detail and follow-through with all instructions is also extremely important. A great Living Trust is worthless unless one properly assigns title to the Living Trust of all the assets. The will does not control the beneficiary of the life insurance policy or retirement asset. These documents also need to be periodically reviewed and updated to keep them working as efficiently as possible with the ever-changing body of law and tax code regulating estates. Marriages, divorces, births, deaths, and changing attitudes will also dictate changes and updates. Imagine the horror of a second spouse watching a life insurance policy or retirement account go to the ex-spouse because a simple beneficiary change was not completed after the divorce.

Example 3: Sometimes the problem arises from a simple lack of planning. It goes without saying that it is important to have a will in place, but it is also important to have an overall estate plan in place as well. The future is very uncertain for all of us, so steps taken to plan in advance provide some degree of peace of mind. The following story never needed to happen, but due to a case of procrastination, much harm was done and unnecessary expense was incurred. The following story comes from a family of four siblings who experienced a rather bizarre situation:

We'll refer to them as the Hunter family. There were four siblings, two sisters and two brothers. When one of the brothers died prematurely of cancer, it was discovered that he had willed all of his rental houses at a beach resort to his oldest sister. However, because he did not have a good estate plan and also because the value of the property had escalated, the estate taxes required by the state were so high that the sister had to sell her business in order to pay them. Later, she had to repossess the business, so eventually things all worked out, but in the meantime she had suffered through much stress and trauma because of a simple lack of planning. She learned firsthand the value of an estate plan—especially when great value is involved.

Because of these unfortunate circumstances, the oldest sister determined to have her affairs in order so that such a thing would never happen with her estate. She had no children, and knowing that her two remaining siblings did not get along, she determined to prepare a new will. She was careful to make arrangements that were appropriate for each sibling, and she also made provisions to keep from causing them similar problems. The new will would have specified the disposition of particular properties, and all would have been settled peacefully. This new will had been prepared for more than three months and simply awaited her signature. However, in spite of all her planning, her unexpected death occurred—*before* she signed the new will. This resulted in the old will being in power—which simply split the estate 50/50 between her two siblings without the protective provisions that had been incorporated into the new will.

One of the siblings had selfish motives and began to hide things from the other, some of which could have had IRS ramifications. The end result was many years in courts fighting over property, and more than half of the money of the estate ended up being spent on legal fees to finally settle this estate.

Example 4: Sometimes people agree to things they don't like "in order to keep the peace." I believe this usually arises from personality differences among siblings. The following example illustrates this well:

Two brothers and a sister get together to settle their parents' estate. One of the brothers has a "take charge" personality and is used to having things done his way. He owns his own company, and he's the boss. The fact that he is the older of the siblings only makes matters worse. The younger brother seems to have an "I don't care" attitude—largely because his personality type views conflict as " not worth the struggle" to disagree with his older brother. The sister has a love for antiques and ancestry. Many things from the estate have little monetary value, but to her they have great sentimental value.

The older brother insists the best thing for all concerned is to have an auction for everything rather than spending the unnecessary time and energy to sort through it all. He argues that the money made from such an auction would allow them to buy anything they might want, and he sees no sense in any other approach.

Younger brother says, "Whatever—I'll go along with whatever you want to do—makes no difference to me." Sister has a personality that hates conflict, and although she is skeptical and has things she wants to keep, it finally seems useless, and she gives in instead of fighting with her brothers.

The result is devastating—and very sad. As a result, nobody has much of anything from the parents to pass along to the next generation or to remember fondly. Though it is true that "things" should not be most important to us, there was no reason for not taking a little extra time and effort to avoid the heartache that followed in years after—especially for the sister, who still harbors resentment toward her older brother.

Note: The option of "selling everything" could also be motivated by the desire for monetary gain when items to be sold are perceived to have a high dollar value. In other words, simply dividing up furniture and other household items would not produce cash assets. This is something to be decided upon within each family estate and can vary greatly depending on the situation at hand for *all* siblings at the time of the settlement. However, if the final disposition of such items is of significant concern, advance planning about how this should be done should probably be designated in a will. Sometimes there are items that have been within a family for generations that a parent may feel should continue to be passed on to the next generation. If they perceive that this succession might be in jeopardy due to circumstances that exist among the immediate heirs, specific designation within a will would be important.

The combinations of situations that cause problems are limitless. The point is that you should consider having a plan in place to achieve a "peaceful and fair" settlement when the time comes. It is important to recognize that there are times when a person has a specific reason to be sure a certain child or other person receives a particular item—that is not what I am referring to here. Of course people have the right to do what they wish to do. However, if you are making an estate plan for the purpose of keeping the peace and preventing family conflict, then I suggest you avoid actions that could cause resentment and conflict between or among your heirs. If it is appropriate, it might be important to discuss your approach openly with your children (or eventual heirs). One of the primary purposes of The Settlement Game is to provide a workable plan for parents to suggest to their heirs as a method to help achieve fairness and openness.

Personality Differences

If you are reading this for the purpose of finding recommendations about how to divide up the material assets of the estate of your parents, you have in your hands a valuable tool to direct you. However, before you start the process, I strongly urge you to consider the personalities of the other heirs who will be involved in this process with you. In Example 4 given earlier in this chapter, there was some discussion about the different personality types of the participating heirs (siblings in this case).

Over the years I have often been asked what I believe causes conflict more than anything else. I am now convinced that personality differences are the primary cause of conflict during an estate settlement. Without understanding these differences, the process of keeping the peace and avoiding conflict will be much more difficult.

I came to this conclusion after having the fortunate opportunity to attend several talks on personality styles given by Dr. Robert A. Rohm of Atlanta, Georgia. After hearing him, and then reading and studying several of his books, I began to discover how important and applicable this information is in all of our relationships. However, as I started the process of writing this book, I realized how beneficial this information would be to those who read the book in anticipation of going through an estate settlement. Therefore, I contacted Dr. Rohm and asked him to contribute information about the personality styles as they apply to the estate settlement process, and he graciously agreed to do so.

Many people are not aware that there are four basic personality styles. Each style sees the world differently. Each style has great strengths, and each style has several weaknesses. To help you understand personality styles, here are Dr. Rohm's words of wisdom paraphrased into a quick overview for our specific purpose:

D: *The Dominant Style* (Outgoing/Task-Oriented people). The basic traits of this personality style are: Dominant, Demanding, Direct, Determined, Decisive, Doer, Dictatorial, Dogmatic, Diligent, Dynamic, and Defiant. They are goal-oriented, performance conscious, hard to please, self-confident, industrious, and firm. They don't like indecision, slow people, talkers who don't produce, lazy people, detailed activities, and taking orders.

Tips for communicating with the "D" personality type are: Think in terms of "What" questions. Get to the main point. Focus on action-based results. Be brief and specific. Be confident. Overcome obstacles. Provide challenge rather than give orders.

I: *The Inspiring Style* (Outgoing/People-Oriented people). The basic traits of this personality style are: Inspirational, Influencing, Inducing, Impressive, Interesting, Impressionable, Interested in people, Imaginative, Impulsive, and Illogical. They are fun to watch, great starters—poor finishers, likable, prone to exaggerate, and easily excitable. They don't like being ignored, being isolated, being ridiculed, repetitive tasks, detail work, or long-term projects.

Tips for communicating with the "I" personality type are: Think in terms of "Who" questions. Let them express their ideas. Keep a friendly environment. Turn talk to action. Focus on their accomplishments. Provide compliments. Gently steer them back to business.

S: *The Supportive Style* (Reserved/People-Oriented People). The basic traits of this personality style are:

Steady, Stable, Secure, Supportive, Servant's Heart, Sweet, Submissive, Shy, Status-quo, Sentimental, Save everything, and Sameness. They are viewed as the sweetest people in the world. However, they are easily manipulated. They are loyal friends and team players. Although they are poor starters, they are great finishers. They don't like insensitivity, to be yelled at, misunderstandings, sarcasm, surprises, or being pushed.

Tips for communicating with the "S" personality type are: Think in terms of "How" questions. Be agreeable and nonthreatening. Give them time to adjust to changes. Show appreciation. Provide follow-up support. Talk more slowly during stress—do not rush the conversation. Demonstrate sincerity.

C: *The Cautious Style* (Reserved/Task-Oriented People). The basic traits of this personality style are: Competent, Cognitive, Cautious, Careful, Calculating, Critical thinking, Compliance wanting, Conscientious, Correct, Conformist, Consistent, and Cold. They are perfectionists, difficult to satisfy, logical, meticulous, self-sacrificing, and inquisitive. They don't like mistakes, sudden changes, shoddy work, lack of preparation, unnecessary interruptions, and being criticized.

Tips for communicating with the "C" personality type are: Think in terms of "Why" questions. Be specific on points of agreement. Avoid emotionalism. Check your facts. Show a "pro and con" balance sheet. Show how they fit in. Provide proof. Patiently welcome questions.

Although every person is a unique creation, knowing the personality style of the people involved in an estate settlement will generally give clues as to how each person thinks and therefore how conflicts may be reduced. Each style sees the world in a different way. For example:

"D's" move quickly and make decisions quickly. They are impatient, and they will probably want to "boss" the process. They have a potential to "run-over" others, and unless they are aware and careful, they may hurt the feelings of others. However, "D's" are the style least likely to hold a grudge after all is finished—no matter what happens.

"I's" are impatient, easily distracted, and easily bored. They like to talk about the work to be done but frequently do not show up for the chores involved in the estate settlement process. They may agree to something and then not follow through. Other heirs may be upset, because they do not feel that the "I" has done his or her part.

"S's" are easygoing and hate conflict. "S's" will generally agree to do more than their share, and other heirs may try to take advantage of them. Their spouse may be anxious to make sure that they get their fair share. In addition, "S's" will probably be the most sentimental heirs.

"C's" are organized and perfectionistic. They will generally be critical of how others handle things. They want things done the "right" way. Many times their idea of the "right" way conflicts with the "right" way ideas of the other heirs. "C's" may want the process to go slower than any of the other heirs.

As you can see, knowledge of personality styles can help you to understand the other heirs more fully and to see potential problems before they arise. As has already been noted, there are both strengths and weaknesses in all personality types. Some people tend to assume other family members view the world the same way they do, and as a result, they hurt the feelings of others easily without ever knowing they have done so. Other people are more sensitive about issues that some don't even realize exist, and as a result, they keep quiet in order to "keep the peace." A simple explanation of their feelings would redirect the process and prevent resentful feelings from surfacing later.

There are numerous possible scenarios; however, I believe that even a basic understanding of personality styles and an understanding of the factors that pertain to each would make a tremendous difference in how people deal with these issues.

Anyone facing an eventual estate settlement or other division of property among several people would greatly benefit from reading the book, *Positive Personality Profiles*, by Dr. Robert A. Rohm. This is an easy read and would also be beneficial to anyone who is dealing with protecting, preserving, or improving any relationship. Moreover, this is especially important during a stressful time, such as an estate settlement, when understanding others and getting along could be critical. You can order this book by Dr. Rohm by using the convenient order form in the back of this book or by going to my website: www.thesettlementgame.com. Click on the SHOP NOW button to access my online store. *Positive Personality Pro-files* as well as other books and resources by Dr. Rohm are available there.

The foreword to Dr. Rohm's book is written by Zig Ziglar, who states: "Communication has been my life. I believe it is the key to happy, healthy relationships, as well as success in the financial world. Dr. Robert Rohm is one of the clearest communicators I have ever heard, and these truths can change your life. I believe in and appreciate the principles found in this book. We use this system in my own company and have profited immensely from it. You are in for a real treat!"

> Perhaps Robert Rohm states it best himself, "If I understand you and you understand me, doesn't it stand to reason that we will be in a position to have a better relationship?"

Finally, the article reprinted following this paragraph caught my eye while I was doing research on the Internet during the writing phase of this manuscript. With permission, I have reprinted it below for your further consideration. Although I fully agree with the statements contained in the article, it is my hope that this book will serve to supply the missing piece within your estate plan as a guide about how to make an even distribution of the assets of the estate. It may also guide you in finding some-one who can further assist you in this important task of Estate Planning.

Don't Let Poor Estate Planning Tear Your Family Apart

(This article originally appeared in the NAEPC newsletter—
National Association of Estate Planners & Councils.)

Even if your kids are grown-up with families of their own, you can probably remember scenes of intense sibling rivalry when they were younger. In some families, that competition continues into adulthood; for others, it recedes as children age and mature. But it can all come flooding back while trying to divide up your estate after your death, as your kids argue over who gets what.

If you die without a will, a court will decide, based on state law, who will inherit your property. In most cases, the result might be contrary to your wishes. Think of all the assets you've accumulated: house, car, jewelry, investments, family heirlooms and more. "It is simply not enough to say 'let them just divide it evenly or work it out themselves,'" says Gerald A. Youngs, president of the National Association of Estate Planners & Councils (NAEPC). This is sure to create problems and expenses due to probate laws, state laws and court appointed strangers making family decisions.

"While many people worry about the federal estate tax, the truth is most of us won't have a tax problem under the current tax laws," says Youngs. "But the 'family tax' is a very real concern," he adds. The family tax is the price paid by children, grandchildren and favorite charities when you do not express your wishes legally. The family tax is paid not only with money, but also with hard feelings.

But it doesn't have to be this way. You can make it easy on you and your family by taking a few simple steps

21

to make sure your estate is in order. Whatever the size of your estate, the first step is to have your intentions put in writing, either in a basic will or a will plus the trust documents that will be needed to carry out your wishes. An estate planning professional can help you make the best decision for your situation.

Once you have a plan in place, discuss it with your family. If anyone has any questions about the details, or any quibbles, you can address them and put to rest any future squabbles. While your family shouldn't dictate your actions, they should be informed about them.

This is also a good time to discuss dividing up personal property. People often arrange for the executor of their will to divide personal property their spouse doesn't want (such as furniture and jewelry) among their children. Simply leaving it at that can cause problems. It is better to put together a list with a description of the property and who you'd like to have it. You can put this list together with input from your children to alleviate any hard feelings later.*

Putting together an estate plan is not as daunting as it might seem at first, and it pays big dividends in the long run. Not having an estate plan in place can cost you not only in dollars and cents, but also in family discord.

If you need help finding specialists in this kind of planning, look for individuals who have earned the designation AEP (Accredited Estate Planner) or EPLS (Estate Planning Law Specialist); ask about the Estate Planning Council members in your area; or call the National

---

* NOTE: See Example 1, page 3. Caution! Perhaps using the methods taught in this book would be even better.

Association of Estate Planners & Councils at (866) 226-2224 (toll free) or visit their Website at www.naepc.org for a referral to a professional near you.

Reprinted by permission from aracontent.com.

Other Suggestions

1. Included in the rules of will-making is the right for you to designate the method to be used in the settlement of your estate. Therefore, you can designate the use of this book, *The Settlement Game*, for the purpose of dividing the material property.

2. When making out your will, give a copy of *The Settlement Game* to each of your heirs *and especially to your executor.*

3. Put a copy of *The Settlement Game* in your safe deposit box or wherever you keep the most current copy of your will and/or your estate plan.

4. Donate a copy of *The Settlement Game* to your church library.

5. Recommend *The Settlement Game* to friends, funeral homes, estate planners, fiduciary lawyers, clergy, antique shops, and others.

6. After reading this book and using it to help divide property, write us about *your* Settlement Game and tell us how this book has helped you.

Voyages Press, Inc.
11193 Big Canoe • Big Canoe, GA 30143
or email: amorris@thesettlementgame.com

Common Sense
Is No Gamble

Our father was Eugene Albert Epting, known to his friends as "Gene," to our mother and his grandchildren as "Ep," and to us (his children) as "Daddy." He was a rather quiet and good-humored man. He was a successful and highly respected trial lawyer, well known for his honesty and ethical integrity. Occasionally he would even teach law ethics at the University of Georgia School of Law. He represented many corporate clients and insurance companies as a defense attorney, and he served as the school board attorney for the Clarke County Board of Education in Athens, Georgia, for more than thirty years.

It was in the capacity of school board attorney that he found himself in position for the distinct honor of arguing a case before the United States Supreme Court. It is perhaps the case for which he was best known: McDaniel v. Barresi, 402 U.S.39 (1971), commonly referred to as the "Busing Case," argued before the Supreme Court of the United States on 13 October 1970, and decided 20 April 1971. A brief summary of that case is presented in the Appendix of this book.

Occasionally he counseled individuals over personal and family matters, such as arguments and conflicts that arose from the process of settling an estate. During his more than fifty years of practicing law, he formed some basic beliefs about the source of such conflicts. Although he naturally recognized the necessary and important role of an attorney in such matters, he also believed that most people could solve their own *relationship* problems of this sort without attorneys if they would just listen to one another and communicate and practice the Golden Rule. He explained this meant that people should treat others as they "would like to be treated," not necessarily as they "have been treated."

> Treat others as you "would like to be treated," not necessarily as you "have been treated."

Throughout our lives, he made it his policy not to discuss the names of clients or details of either his court cases or his professional dealings with people. But sometimes he would reflect on some of the more humorous situations or make suggestions about ways in which people could have avoided unnecessary legal complications through the use of ordinary *common sense*.

From his legal perspective, he felt that family members often engaged in unnecessary squabbling while trying to settle an estate. He would suggest ways in which he felt these conflicts could be avoided. The overall plan, which ultimately became called *The Settlement Game*, was inspired by his teachings. He recommended a procedure using a deck of cards to draw for the material possessions of an estate. We decided to use dice for this instead, as will be explained later in this book.

> *The Settlement Game* is a way to divide and settle an estate peacefully and fairly.

These pages will detail many of the suggestions and principles our father recommended, which further evolved during the actual settlement of our parents' estate in 1993–94. It is a way to settle an estate peacefully (without conflict) and fairly (so that things are evenly divided). It can also be a lot of fun. It suggests a bit of his humor and reflects his love for games. It may seem like a "gamble" for the moment, but in the long run it provides a fair and equitable way to divide both money and possessions that have not specifically been designated in a will, especially among surviving children (or immediate heirs). However, this procedure could easily be altered for use in other circumstances, such as in dissolving business partnerships, divorces, retirement and withdrawal from a business venture, or any other situation requiring the division of material possessions.

Stories from our personal experiences are included to illustrate certain points. If you have questions about something, please keep reading. You will most likely find everything explained satisfactorily by the time you have finished. In order to be fair and to protect our relationships with each other, we developed systems of organization for the overall process. These are also documented herein to assist you further.

Since our purpose was to divide and settle the estate peacefully, we decided that the best approach to this was to make sure we all agreed upon the rules from the outset. Having systems of organization in place ensured that everyone would be on the same page. The next chapter will assist you in making some important decisions and preparations before you actually begin the process of settling an estate.

3

The Ground Rules

There are some preliminary matters that should be discussed and a few steps of preparation to make before taking other action toward the settlement of the estate:

1. Determine the Players

Only heirs or beneficiaries should be involved in the settlement of the estate or "playing" *The Settlement Game*. All outside influences, such as spouses, children of heirs, in-laws, grandchildren, and family friends, should *not* be involved or allowed to participate at the beginning phase of this process.

Our father had an opinion that "many of the problems that would arise at the time of a division or settlement of an estate were caused by the interference from spouses or children of heirs, not the heirs themselves." This opinion was formed through his personal observations as an attorney for more than fifty years. He had dealt with many families and situations throughout his career.

2. Commit to a Common Goal to Achieve a Peaceful and Fair Settlement

Regardless of past experiences or the state of family relationships, it is important at the beginning of the process for all "players" to agree on the following common goal: *To achieve a peaceful and fair settlement.* There are often vast differences among heirs that could easily cause conflict without this commitment. As discussed in Chapter 1, personality differences often account for many of the problems that develop in settlements. Because the four of us had very different personalities, our own family situation will serve to illustrate this point very well:

There are four of us—female, female, male, female. I am the second daughter. One sister is six-and-a-half years older and the other sister is six-and-a-half years younger. My brother is almost three years younger than I. With about thirteen years between the oldest and the youngest, we almost represented three different generations. Our interests, hobbies, and personalities are different. At the time of the settlement, our respective lifestyles and circumstances of life were quite different as well. As you will see from the following descriptions, we had very little " in common" among us, except perhaps for our value system.

My older sister has two boys. At the time of this settlement, both of them were grown (29 and 25), away from home, and already on their own. She was an "empty nester." She and her husband were beginning to make decisions about retirement, building a new home, and moving.

My two boys were both teenagers (15 and 13) and deeply involved in sports and learning to drive. My husband and I were dealing with the challenges of teenagers in the house, while struggling with both time and the financial pressures of business. While I was involved in the day-to-day operation of our businesses, my husband worked 12- to 14-hour days teaching history and coaching football and other sports at the local high school.

My brother's three children were very young (9, 7, and 6) and involved in early elementary school and other activities. He was still at the young child-care stage of life. He was living outside of Georgia working as the director of an area YMCA. His family was in great turmoil and confusion as they were anticipating a move back to the Athens area or another location in Georgia.

Finally, my younger sister was not yet married but had met her future husband. At the time of our parents' death, she had just become engaged and was going through the process of planning a wedding and then establishing her new home out West. By the time we actually reached the division stage, her wedding was only a few months away.

Where we lived and how we lived were equally diverse. My older sister lived in the metro Atlanta area, in an upscale suburban neighborhood. I lived in Evans, Georgia, outside of the Augusta area, in the middle of a small tract of land with a pond and a barn. My brother lived in Knoxville, Tennessee, in a townhouse but was anticipating a move. And finally, my younger sister was living in Crested Butte, Colorado.

Even our majors in college reflect our very different personalities. My older sister majored in English. I majored in geography and cartography. My brother majored in recreation, and my younger sister majored in journalism.

The four Epting heirs with parents and families in 1989 at the retirement party for their father. Shown left to right— Front Row: Fae Epting Davidson, Jean Epting Mosshart, Angie Epting Morris (author), Eugene Albert Epting, Frances Thomas Epting; Top row: Roger Mosshart, Al Epting, Carter Morris, Hunter Morris, Taylor Morris

There is an important reason for this discussion about our differences. Our relationships with each other had never been very close while we were growing up, and at this point our lifestyles were very different. Although we all wanted to believe we had a close family, obviously we had our share of differing opinions. We represented the ideal climate for the development and growth of problems. In addition, the emotions surrounding the loss of both parents within three months of one another could easily have exacerbated these differences and erupted into discord during the process of settling our parents' estate.

In spite of our differences, we all came to an agreement: We wanted to create a process that would allow us to settle everything peacefully and fairly. We became committed to preventing any hard feelings. We wanted to end up still friends when the process was complete. What eventually happened gave us far more than we anticipated or expected...we actually became close friends!

3. Agree Not to Remove Anything from the Home or Premises

Even before reaching a point of making decisions about how to divide anything, there is a critical preliminary rule to follow. It is very important that nothing be removed from the home or business or other property prior to the official division. This rule should be in effect even prior to the death of the parents if such is anticipated.

This rule refers to removing anything one wants. Although it may seem harmless, the act of taking something seems to be a major source of damage to relationships in the estate settlement process. However, a word of caution about this "removal of property" issue is in order. Sometimes common sense is required, as illustrated in the following example:

EXAMPLE: After the death of our father, we agreed to pack up the silver and valuable jewelry and to remove them to my sister's home for safekeeping. We had rotating nurses providing care for our mother who was critically ill. Although we trusted those whom we knew, we didn't have complete control over who came and went from the house at this stage. All of us lived outside of Athens at the time, and we felt that this step was necessary—even if only to remove the temptation. After our mother's death, we brought these items back so they could first be included in the household appraisal and then ultimately in the division process.

4. Establish a System of Organization
(This System is discussed in detail in Chapter 4—The Game Setup.)

Looking back, I am sure this endeavor brought us all forever closer together and even served to bridge many gaps and smooth over our obvious and potential differences. The remainder of this book will present step-by-step procedures to guide you in establishing a system of organization to fit *your* individual circumstances. Although it takes many pages to describe all the details, the actual process of setting it up will not take very long, and certainly it is worth any time and effort needed. (*Note:* The Settlement Game Organization Kit could further help to make this setup quick and easy. See the order form at the end of this book.)

These four Ground Rules are so very important. Incorporate them into whatever you decide to do. They will make a great difference in the final outcome.

1. Determine the players (heirs only)
2. Commit to a common goal of keeping peace in the family
3. Agree not to remove anything from the premises
4. Establish a system of organization

We regarded this as a fun game. We brought back many great memories while sharing this process. But like any game, in order for it to be fair, all participants must know and agree upon the rules, and then all must play by them.

4

The Game Setup

At the outset, it is important to decide who is the one person (heir, family member, beneficiary, executor, etc.) who has the best organizational skills or business background. Appoint this person to be the official record keeper for the entire process. (*Note:* This does not necessarily have to be the executor of the will. Often it will be the same person, but not always. Also, there may be more than one heir who excels at keeping records and possesses exceptional organizational skills. Every situation is different, but if this is a concern, perhaps the two could share responsibilities by dividing the tasks that need to be handled between them.)

There are several important things to do at this point. It is worth the effort to do these things before trying to settle or divide the estate. Acquire the necessary supplies for recording the information—things as simple as a notebook with looseleaf paper, a few pencils with good erasers, a small cash box, and some basic office supplies. (*Note:* The Settlement Game Organization Kit is available for purchase through the order form at the end of this book. It contains all of the supplies and forms needed for the process discussed throughout this book.)

> **It is extremely important that accurate records be kept!**

Things to do and forms to use:

Appraisal—Hire a professional appraiser to come in to make a list of every item that has a significant monetary value, and assign a dollar value to each item. Be sure to get this in written form with recognizable descriptions for each item. (*Note:* Use the actual descriptions of items, not a numbering system. A numbering system assigns each item a number as in a catalog. Such will have no meaning years later.) There will be a cost for this service, but it is well worth it. Pay for this from the estate. Furthermore, if at all possible in your area, hire the services of an appraiser who will give you a "flat price" for this service as opposed to a percentage basis. Although it's not always the case, some appraisers will value items higher to provide a positive impact on their fee if they are using a percentage method. If you can only find appraisers who use the percentage method, negotiate a "fee cap" at the very least, and do so before you make any agreements with them. There are reputable services available for this. Ask for recommendations from legal counsel or from financial planners or others whom you trust. It would be wise to request a list of references from any appraiser you are considering. Be sure to check the references thoroughly. A good appraiser is worth a great deal in this process—so find one who is reputable and ethical.

As a bonus for having such an appraisal done, you will most likely discover a few surprises in the value of some things you did not realize had much value at all. In our process, our appraiser discovered several such items. For example, several small items that we had seen around the house our entire lives had value beyond our wildest dreams. There was a very small cloisonné vase that was worth a great deal—something we even questioned as to having any worth at all. Another such item was a Roseville pottery dish that wasn't even very attractive to me. (However, after learning of its value, it became much more attractive than before my enlightenment.)

> *Everything* depends on this appraisal, so take the time and spend the money it requires to do this.

To hire a professional appraiser, you may wish to shop among those listed in your area who are affiliated with either the American Society of Appraisers (ASA) or the Appraisers Association of America (AAA). These organizations have a code of ethics and abide by the Uniform Standards of Professional Appraisal Practice (USPAP) set forth by the Appraisal Foundation in Washington. In order to become a certified member of either of these organizations, candidates must prove their qualifications through both evaluative efforts and examinations to show technical appraisal proficiency. Both associations have a membership directory. For online information, including how to find members in your region, go to one of the following websites: American Society of Appraisers, www.appraisers.org, or Appraisers Association of America, Inc., www.appraisersassoc.org. (NOTE: A form for this purpose appears in the Appendix.)

Interest Lists—Before any dividing begins, have each of the participants make a list of any items to which they have a claim or in which they have a particular interest. For each item listed, a brief explanation should be given for why the item is wanted or why one feels it can be claimed. (Sometimes the reasons may be as simple as "because they had previously given the item as a gift to the deceased parent," etc.) This should be done by each heir privately, and the number of items of this sort should be limited to perhaps five each (ten at the most). The heirs should then meet to decide about these items of special interest before going forward. If the item is uncontested and all can agree without a problem, then that heir gets the item requested. If any item begins to foster dispute or controversy, even in a friendly manner, or if one of the other heirs has also listed that item, it goes back into the general pool, which will be discussed later.

> EXAMPLE: Perhaps the best example of this from our experience involved an antique christening gown that had been handmade by our great-grandmother for our maternal grandmother's christening in 1881. The same gown had also been worn by our mother and her three sisters

A good example of this for us involved an antique christening gown that had been handmade by our great-grandmother for our maternal grandmother's christening in 1881.

and then by the four of us in our generation and finally by our children, so it represented four generations. This was the top item on my list, because I wanted to be able to pass it down to my youngest son, who had been the last to wear it for his christening in 1981, exactly 100 years after it was made and first worn by our grandmother. Although the gown had no declared monetary value, it held senti-mental value for all of us. It was agreed that I should have the gown for my son, so without any controversy, I re-ceived it.

Important Note: If the item has a declared value, that amount is credited to the heir who receives the item. This procedure is partially described in the following paragraph and will be further explained later in Chapter 7—Keeping Score. (NOTE: A form for this purpose ap-pears in the Appendix.)

Distribution Sheets—Make a sheet for each heir or participant. Each item selected should be listed in one column by description, with the monetary value listed in an adjacent and corresponding column. (Use the list from the appraiser for this task.)

This listing process is essential to achieving an "equal" division of property. Be sure to recognize how important it is always to record each item with its corresponding monetary value assigned. Also, from our experience, we discovered that it is vital to record each item immedi-ately when it is selected. No matter how good intentions are, it is easy to forget or to skip something if things are not done in this order.

> It is vital to record each item immediately when selected.

Other Items of Organization

(not presented in any particular order)

Receipts—All participants should document and keep receipts of any expense incurred related to the settlement process. These should be given to the person appointed as the record keeper in order that eventual reimbursement can be made. This should be done on an agreed upon schedule to avoid any chaos and confusion and to relieve pressure on the person disbursing the funds. (We chose to settle monthly.) Only the appointed person should ever disburse funds. Payments of these reimbursements should always be made by check from the estate account so that there is a clear record of the payment.

Expenditures Cap—All expenditures over a specified amount must be approved by the other participants before obligation or payment. We set our limit at $500, but the amount should be agreed upon, whatever it is. Of course, all disbursements, no matter how small, must be fully documented and accounted for by the appointed record keeper. No action resulting in an expense over $500 was ever made without the full consent of all participants or heirs *before* purchase or contract and payout.

Petty Cash Fund—We decided to keep at least $100 in a petty cash fund at the house for use as needed by us in the settlement process. It was often used for cleaning or office supplies, fast food for lunch and other minor expenses. The money was taken from the estate account and was replenished as needed.

Petty Cash Receipts—For miscellaneous expenses, we always put a receipt in the petty cash box with further description on it telling what it was for, our name, and the date. In this way, no one ended up paying more than their share, and all was fair. This prevents any one participant from taking advantage of the others, even unintentionally. In this way the estate ends up paying for the minor and petty things that the settlement process requires. It is often the little things that cause the problems, so this is just one more simple process that prevents minor misunderstandings from becoming major problems.

Travel Allowances—If the settlement process extends over a long period of time and requires some of the participants to travel from a distance away in order to be present for something related to the settlement, you may wish to assign a travel allowance to each participant for the round-trip expenses.

> EXAMPLE: In our case, all of us were living outside of town at the time of the settlement of the estate. Since the place for settlement was our parents' home in Athens, Georgia, we all had to travel from our respective homes in Atlanta; Augusta; Knoxville; and Crested Butte, Colorado. We agreed to pay for two round-trip airline tickets for our sister in Colorado. One of these was for her to come for some time at the beginning of the process, and the second was

for her to come when the actual division process took place. The other three of us calculated the expense of driving by deciding on a per-mile rate. By multiplying that rate by the number of round-trip miles, we arrived at a compensation figure particular to each of us individually. In 1994 when we did this, we used the mileage rate of 25 cents per mile. For instance, round-trip from Augusta was 200 miles times 25 cents per mile. Thus, I was reimbursed $50 for every round-trip I made to be present for something related to the process. Many of my trips related to preparation before we actually began the division process. This involved some major cleaning and sorting through stacks of things and boxes of old papers and magazines. Often it required figuring out "unknowns." Since my older sister and I were more available than the other two siblings to do this, the mileage reimbursement made it a fair solution to what could have caused us to feel we were being required to do more than our share.

Every situation will be different and should therefore be dealt with at the beginning to set up the individual procedures and rules that will apply. We felt it was extremely important to come to a mutual consent about all of these things before we started.

5

Preparing the Field of Play

A Few Other Valuable Suggestions

The following are some things we did that may be helpful to you in starting this process. These are not presented in any special order nor will everything here apply in every situation. Like everything else presented in this book, take what is here as something to help you think of things you can do. My hope is that these ideas will help you prevent problems.

As we began the process, we spent a great deal of time sorting through things and organizing. One of the first things we did was to clean out several drawers in the family room and designate a drawer for each of us. Then as we would find something like a newspaper article or a picture, etc., that was specifically about one of us, we would put it into that person's drawer. As these began to fill, we would go through our individual drawers and either discard or remove the items to file in our own way and remove them from the house.

We took time to do some interesting things that proved to be great fun. We found many stray pieces of board games scattered throughout the house in various drawers and other unusual places. Just for fun, we began reconstructing many of these games, and before we were finished, we had put back together several games such as Monopoly, Candy Land, and so forth.

Another thing we did was to designate a drawer in which to put any pieces of broken furniture or items that appeared to be important—as if they had been saved for a reason. We were amazed at the number of things we were able to put back together or mend because of this— things that had apparently been broken for years! If time does not permit such, these things will have to be dis-carded as you go.

We approached the entire procedure as a cleaning-out process. We tackled one room at a time, and we went through *everything*—every drawer, cabinet, closet, box, etc. We kept trash bags on hand, and we threw out tons of stuff as we went but only after making sure we all agreed that it was truly trash. In many cases, we found someone outside the family who could use things that were still good but not wanted or needed by any of us. We returned many things to people that we found or offered items to friends and neighbors of our parents.

Since family friends were often involved, we had a real opportunity to say goodbye. This proved to be a re-warding and healing time for all of us and often elicited stories about our parents that we will treasure always but that we might not ever have heard had we not done this.

There is no way to put a price tag on things of this sort that occurred as a result of giving away much of the stuff that otherwise would have been thrown out due to a lack of usefulness or monetary value.

Early in the process we began to collect quite an assortment of old photographs. It quickly became evident that every picture our parents had taken had been saved. There were also many photographs, probably of family members, that we could not identify. We collected these in one of our boxes (discussed on page 52). Then, whenever older relatives came by, we would ask questions and try to have them look through the old pictures and give us as much information as they could about who, what, when, where, or why. We wrote this information on the backs of the photographs. Since our daddy died three months before our mother, at first we had a situation similar to most families—one parent was deceased, and the other was still living in the home. We did not begin this process at all as long as our mother was still alive. This was mostly out of respect for her. If the situation allows, it might be appropriate to begin this photo identity process with elderly parents before they are gone. There is a good chance they will recall not only the names but the date and circumstances of many of the photos you find.

Something I did with many of those old pictures has proven to be a lot of fun. It is something you might want to do with some of your old pictures of relatives. If you can identify many of the direct relatives (parents, grandparents, and even great-grandparents,) perhaps you can frame these to create an "Ancestor Picture Wall." (See picture on the next page.) Even if you don't have pictures from very far back, you can still create one with those available to you. I put ours in our dining room, and in the years that have followed, during meals, much discussion has transpired about these ancestors and about our family. It is a great tool for teaching the family heritage to children or even grandchildren. It creates dinner conversation for other guests as well. Other variations on this idea are of course possible.

If there are old pictures that all heirs want, this problem can be solved easily. Simply collect any pictures desired by all and have copies made for those who want them. Attach a note to each original indicating the number of copies needed. When settling my parents' estate, we had this done by a professional photographer who was also able to improve the quality of some of the older photographs. However, in today's world, with good equipment readily available in such places as Kinko's, Wal-Mart, or other such locations, you can easily handle this task with relatively little expense.

The process of cleaning up created a lot of trash. One thing should absolutely be remembered: *Don't throw anything away*—unless it is truly "trash." Just about everything has value to someone. At the end of the division, you may want to have an outdoor yard sale. If so, we suggest you use a professional service to price items— or you can do it yourself. If you choose to do this, you may even want to invite family friends to come by early for "first choice" of items for sale. Or you could auction off the items not wanted by any of the heirs.

If you can identify many of the direct relatives (parents, grandparents, and even great-grandparents), then perhaps you can frame these individually to create an "Ancestor Picture Wall."

After the sale, you can take all remaining items to charity. If you do so, be sure to get a receipt for each heir by dividing the total value equally. This could be worth from $350 to $500 each in most cases. We chose to do this mainly with clothes.

For true trash we kept a pickup truck available that was owned by a family member. It made numerous trips to the landfill with things that were beyond recognition or repair. Just for fun, we kept track of the tonnage we threw away, and it would amaze you! We also kept track of the expenses of these hauls and reimbursed those in our monthly settlement when we made disbursements. Before you begin hauling, be sure to check on the charges and time schedule for the county landfill closest to the home.

We created several boxes labeled with the names of our parents, grandparents, significant family friends, and any other major category—such as old pictures or financial records—that emerged. In this way, as we found newspaper articles or items while we were sorting, we could quickly file them as related to that person or category. These boxes could be moved about and then used to transport items that had been deposited in them to the more stationary locations, such as the drawers mentioned earlier. This method also allowed us to stack the boxes to the side without disrupting the filing and sorting we had done when we were finished for that day. We didn't have to leave piles of papers and stuff stacked all over the floor. You might say it gave us a portable system of organization. And by the way—you don't have to go buy boxes. Just go to your grocer and ask for "milk cartons." These are sturdy square cardboard boxes with handles that make them convenient for this purpose. Or, if you prefer, banker's boxes can be purchased for a nominal cost. Whatever you use, be sure the containers are the same size to allow for ease in stacking and organizing.

This may sound silly, but we took great pride in leaving the house as clean and orderly as possible every time we left after having completed a session of sorting and filing. This gave us the feeling that we were truly making great progress and getting things in order. It also made starting the next time a bit easier and gave us a quiet refuge to come into every time we returned to the house. This had been our only home as a family, and we wanted to remember it at its best long after we were through. In some cases, the condition of the home may not matter so much. I mention it here because when people care enough to make an extra effort to prevent hurt feelings, it would seem that it might be important.

The issue of leaving the house clean and orderly might prove to be more important to some personality styles than others. For example, as discussed in Chapter 1, a "D" personality style (Outgoing/Task-Oriented) might see this as a pure waste of time. However, a "C" personality style (Reserved/Task-Oriented) sees organization and thoroughness as a must. They want things done the "right" way.

We took time to leaf through every book and even every magazine. We found several special articles and meaningful handwritten notes and even a fair amount of money.

> EXAMPLE: One article we found that would otherwise have been lost to us forever concerned how our daddy had hosted a special "Victory Dinner" in Athens for the son of Franklin D. Roosevelt. Mr. Roosevelt was representing his father after his reelection as president. At that time Daddy was a member of the Georgia legislature. We would never have known about the event because it had never been discussed as far as we knew. The article described quite an affair with a black-tie dinner, many known dignitaries of the day, etc. But more importantly for us, it was an impressive article about our daddy. It would have been thrown away, and we would never have known about it had we not taken the time to go through everything thoroughly.

Another thing we did just for fun was set aside a box for loose cash we found around the house. To our surprise, it turned into a rather impressive fund for "pocket change"—more than $500! Once we were certain that everything in the house had been sorted through and categorized, we split the cash four ways.

6

Playing the Game

Once copies of the *Appraisal* have been distributed to all heirs and *Interest Lists* have been prepared and items listed decided upon, the "Division Process" can begin. Start with a process of grouping items together in numbers that can be divided evenly by the number of heirs participating.

> EXAMPLE: There were four of us dividing our parents' estate. We grouped 16 or 20 items together (numbers divisible by 4). This provided many selections within each grouping.

Grouping

It is best to form only one grouping at a time. Be sure to select items with similar values, starting with those that have the highest value or that are of highest interest first. For example, we grouped the more valuable pieces of antique furniture together first. All of these had similar values. Since there was not a large number of such pieces, this meant that our first grouping was smaller than those that followed.

We worked from the most valuable pieces in our first group down to those with the least value. Many of the items at the end of this process were close to the "junk" level. However, even though there were many things that had no cash value, some of them were well worth keeping for sentimental reasons. Today, many of the things from the estate that I enjoy most are simple things without major cash value, such as some pieces of antique lace. Just knowing my grandmother made a tablecloth that I have on a table in the hall is very special. Or using a piece of handmade lace under a special dish on display on a shelf adds a very cozy touch to my home and also gives me a great sense of belonging and enjoyment.

These are the things that remind me of the warm and pleasant memories of past experiences in my childhood home. They are the loving memories of dreams and

Just knowing that my grandmother made a tablecloth that I have on a table in the hall is very special. Or using a piece of handmade lace under a special dish on display on a shelf adds some very cozy touches to my home and also gives me a great sense of belonging and enjoyment.

Tablecloth made by my grandmother.

aspirations from childhood that allow me to keep a piece of my own family history to pass on to my children. They may even emerge as the most special keepsakes that come from an estate settlement, and they provide great satisfaction and meaning long after the settlement has been completed.

Note: This is an important circumstance where personality differences may be more obvious. It is important for dominant personality types to be patient and understanding with more sensitive and sentimental personality types.

As stated earlier, group items with similar dollar values and keep the groupings in numbers evenly divisible by the number of participants in the dividing process. Unless there are a number of items that are alike or very similar, separate groupings for like kind should not be formed. An example of what might be an exception to this would be a dining room table with sixteen matching chairs, but only eight of the chairs are to be part of the dining room "set," leaving eight additional chairs to be divided. Some of the groupings we formed were obvious, but others were unusual. You can be creative with your groupings. Remember—you are creating your own Settlement Game.

Rolling the Dice

You can roll dice to determine the order in which heirs pick items from the groups. The one who rolls the largest number gets first pick from the first grouping. The person with the second largest number gets second choice and so on for the first round of selections. Although not necessary, it might be nice to have one die per heir (die is singular of dice). If there are six heirs or fewer, each will need only one. If there are seven or more heirs, a pair of dice per participant would be needed.

When the dice are rolled, they should be left on the table in front of the person who rolled them. In this way, there will never be a question about who rolled what number. If there are ties, there may need to be a "roll-off." At first we rolled the dice for each round, but we quickly decided to let the roll of the dice at the beginning of each grouping determine the order of selections for that entire grouping. In other words, we only rolled the dice once at the beginning of each grouping and used that same order until we decided to regroup. *Note:* If time permits, you could continue to roll for each round if that is preferred.

Regrouping

If after two or three rounds in the first grouping the heirs all agree they want to regroup, the unselected items remaining in the grouping should then be regrouped with other items to form a new grouping of selections.

> EXAMPLE: At first we grouped together the more valuable pieces of furniture, which included an antique china cabinet, an antique sideboard, our grandmother's dining room table, and the mahogany table and chairs that we used for meals during the years when we were growing up. Because these and a few other such pieces were of greater value than other items from the estate, we only put eight items in the first grouping. After only one round, we all agreed we would prefer to put the remaining four items into a new grouping, rather than be forced to choose among them. We then formed a group of sixteen items, which also included the four items remaining from the first round. Usually the few remaining items of a grouping will easily blend into the next group of selections.

Make sure the number of items in each grouping can be divided evenly by the number of participants.

Continue in this manner of grouping, rolling the dice, and selecting in order for the number of rounds in that grouping. Then regroup, roll the dice again, select, regroup, roll the dice, select, etc.

EXAMPLE: After we had gone through several rounds and had selected most of the important items, we gathered all the "knickknack" items from all over the house and put them on the dining room table—some one hundred or more in number. We then rolled and selected from this large pool. We continued to do this until nobody wanted anything else. Occasionally one of us would declare there was nothing more that he or she wanted, and withdrew from further participation in this grouping. Then those left would continue without that member until all were finished. If items still remained, we had designated an area to put them to be disposed of at the final step (to be described later).

Color-Coded Tags

Each participant was assigned a color. We also put our names on our tags or stickers to avoid any possible confusion. After a piece of furniture was selected, we tagged it but allowed it to remain in its place in the house without further disruption. This avoided the confusion that would have been caused by moving the item out of the house at the time of selection. We continued with the process until it was completed. We used a combination of colored stickers and paper tags with strings attached. For some items it was appropriate simply to apply a colored sticker. For items where a sticker was insufficient, could cause damage, or would not adhere, we attached a paper tag to the item with a string and put a sticker on the tag to indicate whose it was. You may even be able to find tags in various colors. Also, if there are many heirs, don't feel you have to find that many colors. You can alter these in a variety of ways to represent more participants. For example, if you have eight instead of four heirs, you could still use tags and stickers with four colors (say, red, blue, yellow, and green). For the fifth through eighth participants, use the same colors with an X placed across the tag or sticker. The possibilities are great. (*Note:* The color coding process is essential if there will be someone other than the heir who will pick up the selected items at a later date. A colored tag with a name helps greatly to avoid confusion.)

Where to Put Selections

Later in the process, we each chose a room or area of a room and moved our smaller selections there. We still left the larger items such as furniture in place until they were removed altogether. As we got into smaller items, we began putting these inside or on top of our furniture selections.

A Word about Old Toys

When you are in the process of sorting through all of the things in an estate settlement, there is likely to be an abundance of old toys if there have been children and then grandchildren in the home. Some of these may have special meaning to individuals, but you may find that although there is sentimental attachment, you don't know what you can do with these items—and so they get tossed out or given away with the final accumulation of "stuff" sold off in bulk as described later in this chapter.

However, you may wish to consider a display of "old toys" in a rec room—or any other place where you gather or entertain. These are wonderful conversation pieces, and often people reflect on remembering having similar items during their childhood. The picture below shows what my older sister did with her collection of these items.

You may wish to consider a display of "old toys" in a rec room —or any other place where you gather or entertain.

What to Do with What Is Left

After everything of worth or that is desired by any one of the heirs has been selected and after all the true junk has been discarded, there will be a certain amount of stuff that is left. It may have some value for someone, but none of the heirs want it. One option previously discussed is to take it to a charity if there is enough to warrant a receipt, which would be helpful for a tax deduction. Another possibility is to have someone come in and offer you a lump sum price for everything left. Then have them come pick it up at a designated time and pay you for it at the agreed price. This cash settlement would then be added back to the estate account for an equal division after all other affairs have been settled.

Caution: Do Not Finalize Yet

Finally, one last rule related to the overall monetary division. *Do not finalize* until all other accounts are paid and all amounts are known, such as cash values on stocks and bonds and insurance policies. It is also important to make sure all bills have been paid in full and that accounts have been closed before any further disbursements are made from the estate. (See Chapter 10—Final Stats: The "To-Do" List on record keeping and taxes.)

Of course, some of this may require assistance from your attorney or other professional advisors. As stated previously, this book does not deal with the important legal aspects of a will or with any resultant legal proceedings. Finally, there is one detail to consider before finalizing.

"This Old House"—Make Repairs on Real Estate to Be Sold

If there is a home or other real estate to be sold, it may be necessary to make some repairs or improvements to the property before it can be marketed. However, remember that it is probably not a good idea to do decorative types of improvements, for usually such will not increase the value of the property. If there are essential repairs needed to prevent ongoing damage, such as a leaking roof, that is what I am referring to in this section. If such must be done, it is very important to pay for these repairs and any other work determined necessary from the funds of the estate prior to closing the sale of real estate.

Do not finalize the division of money before paying for the completion of all such work. To do so could cause additional and unnecessary friction among heirs or participants if there are unforeseen expenses, especially if the heirs or participants are later expected to contribute or assist with such expenses. If for any reason one or more of the heirs is unable to do so, it could cause stress and strain on relationships, which is the very thing you are trying to avoid. All the good that might have been achieved through using the methods and principles outlined in *The Settlement Game* could be undone by a hasty finalization and distribution of the funds before all of the details have been wrapped up.

7

Keeping Score

Recording the Value

This step refers back to Chapter 4, where I mentioned the use of distribution sheets to record all monetary values of selections. Each time a selection is made, the item should be added to the Distribution Sheet for that heir, giving both its description and the monetary value assigned to it. I remind you to do this immediately upon selection of each item as discussed previously.

(*Note:* Not all items will have a monetary value—especially as you begin to get to the end of the process. There are probably going to be many more sentimental items and keepsakes at that stage.)

The Tally and Property Equalization

This is the step that makes the entire procedure fair to everyone involved. It is what makes this process work. Be sure to read it, understand it, and apply it!

Note: This step is also why the record-keeping parts are so very important!

After all the groupings are complete and all selections made, it is important to tally the dollar value for each participant. You can use the Tally Sheet for this purpose. (NOTE: This form appears in the Appendix.) Then the list with the highest monetary value can be used as the baseline for the others.

Before any money from the estate is divided in any other manner, it is used to balance out the lists so that each participant receives an equal compensation related to the material things and property in the estate. The heir with the highest dollar value gets no additional monetary compensation at this stage of the division or settlement. All other participants are paid from the estate an amount that makes the value of their list of selections equivalent to the dollar amount of the participant with the highest value. This is better explained in the example that follows.

EXAMPLE: (In this example, assume four heirs are involved in the division.) Let's say that Heir A has the highest value on her list, which equals $10,000 when the values of the selections chosen by A are tallied.

Next, all of the other heirs will be awarded amounts of money from the estate in order to bring their values up to that $10,000 level.

a. If Heir B has a value of $7,000 on his list, Heir B will receive a payment of $3,000 from the estate.

b. If Heir C has a value of $6,000 on her list, Heir C will receive a payment of $4,000 from the estate.

c. If Heir D has a value of $9,000 on his list, Heir D will receive a payment of $1,000 from the estate.

This settlement should take place *before* any other disbursement from the estate in order to equalize the value of the division of the material property. After this step, all further division of money can be disbursed equally among the heirs.

Optional Enhancements to the Game

The following stories tell a little bit about our own situation and what we did before selling our parents' home. In today's world, many people move about regularly as required by jobs, so making a break with a "family home" is not always an issue or difficult task. However, in many situations, there is a home that is hard to part with, and there are memories associated with it that make it difficult to sell the property. Some information about what we did will perhaps help by suggesting some things that might make it easier to let go and finalize a sale.

Our father built our home before he married and moved our mother into it as a bride in 1939. As the family grew, our parents added onto the house more than once, but they remained at the same address for the entire 54 years of their married life together. When a home is this much a part of a family identity, a little extra effort will help to leave everyone with fond memories. This entire process is intended to create happy memories, so the following ideas are some things to do to help make that happen.

You would most likely want to do the things listed below *before* all of the division process takes place. However, they would ideally be done *after* the cleaning and sorting has been completed, so that the house will be in optimum condition. The timing might vary depending on the speed with which this process must be completed.

1. Have One Last Party at the Home

When I was an early teen, my parents built a major addition to our house. Afterward, our home became one of the gathering places for my group of friends. It was here that we had parties, and it was especially known by my friends as the place where we had "spend the night" parties growing up.

Therefore, once my sisters, brother, and I had finished sorting through all the papers and cleaning out the house—yet before we engaged in the actual division of property —I asked permission of my sisters and brother to have one last party in the house. Of course, I assured them that I would get everything in order and clean the house both before and afterward.

I set a date on a weekend and then prepared an invitation to send to friends, inviting them to a "drop-in." Also, I planned to have one last "spend the night" party afterward for my closer girlfriends. Many friends showed up for the "drop-in," and we had such a nice evening with people we had not seen in many years.

Then, after most of the guests had departed for the night, several of my lifelong girlfriends did in fact "spend the night." We stayed up half the night talking, just like we had done so many years before. About the only thing that changed was the topic of conversation—from boyfriends and teenage gossip to husbands and children and even *grand*children!

2. Make a Video of the House and Grounds

This is something I did that has brought me a great deal of satisfaction. Just before my guests arrived for the drop-in, I went through the house and straightened up everything possible and turned on appropriate lighting. I made sure the fresh flowers were arranged and even turned music on to provide the right atmosphere. Then, I walked outside of the house with my video camera and filmed our home, entering through the back door as we had always done while growing up there.

Then, I toured the entire house with the video camera running and provided appropriate narration about each room and certain other things. I kept the camera running as I moved from room to room and even as I walked up the stairs to the bedrooms above. By doing this, I captured our home for posterity.

The next year at Christmastime, among other parts of videos of our family, I included that tape on a composite video to give to each of my siblings for Christmas. It means a great deal to be able to go revisit our home in this manner. Also, it has let us show our children so they too can be reminded of the happy memories they have of that place and of my parents who lived there through their entire married life together.

If there are happy memories related to a home, I highly recommend such a video, even if it must be done in haste and even if you cannot take the time to clean thoroughly beforehand. It is something that will remind you of life as you once knew it, and at times, that can be helpful and comforting in a time of loss or just for the sake of happy memories.

3. Make a Final Photo of the House

Frame pictures of the house together: "Early" and "Last." This is something my older sister did and gave to each of us at Christmas one year. The idea is to capture the home from an old photograph when it was first occupied and then get a good photo of it as it was at the end. This might be particularly meaningful if a home is lived in for many years, as was the case with our parents. My sister had these two photographs mounted and framed. This is very special to each of us—and oddly enough, it arouses much interest from visitors in my home because of its uniqueness and personal value.

A picture like this might be particularly meaningful if a home is also the childhood home of the heirs or was lived in for many years, as was the case with our parents.

9

Overtime Play

As we worked our way through the division of our parents' estate, we didn't realize we were creating something that would eventually end up being offered to the world as a useful method for dividing an estate without conflict. We were simply trying our best to honor our parents by keeping peace in the family. With that goal in mind, we also decided to take this one step further with some agreements at the end of the process that we thought might be important for the future.

We considered the fact that life would go on and that we would each go our separate ways back to our families and our lives—still different from each other in lifestyles and our stages in life. We also realized that each of us had received some special possessions that had belonged to our parents and had been part of our heritage. Because of that, we discussed a plan for the future. As time moves on, people change, situations change, and it is only natural to do what life requires of you. Knowing this, we decided on a plan for the disposal of items that had come from the estate in case any one of us felt the need or desire to get rid of them. Following is that plan. It is presented here to help you think of the long-range effects of all of your actions. Remember: It is the primary goal of this process to keep peace in the family. That means on-going as well as during the actual settlement process.

Keep peace in the family.

---

1. We agreed to notify all the other heirs (i.e., siblings) if there were items that we wanted to dispose of or sell. By doing so, we were giving "right of first refusal" to the others. If more than one had an interest, we determined to find an agreeable way to determine who would get the item. It might mean offering a price by secret bid, or even rolling the dice for the highest number as we had done in the original division.

EXAMPLE: Recently my younger sister moved to another town in Colorado. In this process (as is often true in a move) she and her husband determined they had too much stuff and that they wanted to get rid of some of it. Her lifestyle does not lend itself to formality, and therefore, much of the oriental antique items were a little out of place in her home anyway. As agreed, she contacted all of us to let us know she had several things she wanted to dispose of—either to us as first choice or to sell if we were not interested. Since there was some interest on our part, she agreed that she would bring these items with her when she returned East for a visit that fall. She brought the items to my older sister's home, where the four of us siblings had dinner together and then met to deal with the things my sister had brought. In the end we bought most of the things available. Several were of no further interest to any of us, and she was therefore free to dispose of them any way possible. This proved to produce a "win-win" situation, because the amount she received from us was most likely more than she would have received had she sold the items by more traditional methods. We were happy because, once again, we were able to retain certain keepsakes in the family. This method is just another suggestion for how to continue to ensure ongoing friendly relationships within a family.

2. We agreed that if there was an assigned value, we would use the price as given in the original appraisal list as a starting price, then we could make offers higher or lower accordingly. Also, if there was no assigned value, we agreed we would negotiate a fair and agreeable price with the person interested in buying that item. In this way, we could effectively pass an item on to another family member in a way in which both would benefit from the transaction.

EXAMPLE: In the original settlement, my younger sister received the antique wicker bassinet that had been used by our mother for each of us when we were infants. Since the older three of us already had all the children we intended to have by the time of this settlement, and since my younger sister was about to get married, it only seemed appropriate that she have this item, even though the others of us had also used the bassinet for our children when they were babies. However, after a few years one of my nephews announced that his wife was expecting their first child. In view of the fact that my younger sister had determined not to have children, my older sister arranged to purchase the bassinet from her and had it shipped back East for use at the birth of this grandchild. They worked it out between them, and all of us were happy to "keep it in the family."

Even though this was between my older and younger sisters, they were both considerate enough of the other two of us to tell us what they were doing to ensure that we all agreed to this process. Of course, we had no objections, but what mattered most was the attempt at keeping communication going and the effort to prevent surprises. Hard feelings can occur later if an heir finds out about such things "after the fact." Up-front communication is always the better plan.

The important thing here was that we all agreed not to dispose of an item from the estate without telling the others. That way, we could "keep things in the family." Although that might not seem important to some members of a family, it might be of great importance to others. This method kept us connected in our resolve to keep peace and to be considerate of each other. The discovery after the fact that someone has disposed of an item of sentimental value sometimes causes resentment years later. If you care enough to go to the trouble to have a peaceful settlement, be sure also to think about preventing problems in the future.

We agreed to notify all the other heirs (i.e., siblings) if there were items that we wanted to dispose of or sell. By doing so, we were giving "right of first refusal" to the others.

10

Final Stats:
The "To-Do" List

In this chapter, I wish to provide you with a number of things that are related to the details and record-keeping side of the estate settlement. Once again, I remind you this book is not intended to replace using your attorney or financial planner for the important legal and financial matters related to the settlement of an estate. Therefore, the items listed below are only offered as suggested things for you to check on to be sure they are appropriately managed or handled.

It is also very important to stress that every state has different laws. Even banks may have different requirements, so do not take anything presented in the following paragraphs as things you must do. It is doubtful that everything mentioned here will apply to everyone. However, it is likely that many of these things should be considered in your final process of settling an estate. Some of these things will obviously apply to everyone.

In the interests of time and simplicity, I have listed them in categories related to a particular label, but again, these are in no particular order. I highly recommend that you consult with your attorney or financial advisor about the items that you must address. Then, the method you use, the documents you must provide, and the regulations that apply will vary from state to state or even from county to county. These things are mentioned here because, of course, there are such matters that must be attended to in every estate settlement, so a book of this sort would not be complete without at least giving you a *To-Do List* of things to check on in your county and state.

A. Death Certificate Copies

Keep in mind that throughout the process, there will probably be a number of times when you will need to submit a copy of the death certificate. Therefore, if probate of a will is involved, be sure to get a sufficient number of certified copies from your attorney or probate court. Your advisor can recommend an appropriate number of these for your individual circumstances after considering all of the things for which one will be required.

B. Banking

Take care of all bank accounts. Create an estate account from which to work with check-writing privileges. (This doesn't mean you have to convert everything into that account.) You will need an account with funds available for check-writing purposes and into which you can make deposits as needed.

(NOTE: The information provided in this section about banking is primarily related to the Probate process . If a Revocable Living Trust is part of the estate plan used, much of the following will be avoided. However, consult with your attorney or financial advisor on these matters.)

1. Keep in mind that at the time of death, most states immediately freeze the deceased person's account and only the executor has access to the account from that point forward.

2. The executor must be the one to go to the bank to create the account. If the executor is not going to be the person writing checks from the bank account, then the executor needs to appoint a person to be the agent. This must be done legally—through the attorney. It usually involves a document entitled "Agent for Executor Agreement." (See item 3-c below.)

3. The documents required to establish an estate account may vary from state to state—or even from bank to bank. You should contact the bank to inquire as to these documents. Some of these might include:
   a. A death certificate
   b. A probated copy of the will
   c. Agent for Executor Agreement: If the executor will not be writing the checks, this legal document appoints an agent to do so. Stipulations about what this person is responsible for or allowed to do will be outlined in this Agreement.
   d. A power of attorney

4. Close bank accounts: Inspect all checks written on all accounts of the deceased. Be sure to go back several months to ensure that all checks that were written have cleared. If not, find out the reason and clear up the matter. Then—and *only* then—close all such bank accounts.

C. Household Accounts

Pay all outstanding bills. If the account can be canceled, be sure to send notice to do so. (Things such as credit cards, magazine subscriptions, memberships, or anything that does not need to be continued for the operation of the household should be canceled.) (*Note:* Do *not* just destroy credit cards—you must cancel them officially. Be sure to keep records of these notifications as proof of the cancellation.) Household accounts that are needed for a home to continue functioning must be continued. These might include such things such as telephone, water, electricity, gas, home insurance, and miscellaneous household accounts.

(*Note:* Sometimes utility accounts have deposits that need to be reclaimed. Check on this just in case.) If there are vehicles that will continue to be used, be sure to continue car insurance until such vehicles are transferred or sold. Be sure to monitor all of these accounts until they are all settled. Keep records of their finalization and a notice from the account stating so. (NOTE: A form for this purpose appears in the Appendix.)

D. Forwarding Address

If the home will be empty, a forwarding address should be provided to the post office for all mail. The heir who would logically receive the forwarded mail should normally be the same person who will be in charge of paying the bills, canceling accounts, etc.

E. Life Insurance Policies

Life insurance policies held by the deceased are immediately redeemable. Normally, simply contact the insurance agent or company with the policy number and other appropriate information for identification and determine what you must send them in order to redeem the policy. If you are not certain of the precise agent, direct contact with the company will suffice. You will probably need a copy of the death certificate, among other things, in this process.

F. Income Taxes

These are still due for whatever income was accrued by the deceased until the time of death. Be sure to file appropriate returns on behalf of the deceased. Discuss this with whomever has prepared the income tax return for the deceased in the past. Or, if that person is unknown, ask your own tax advisor or attorney for recommendations.

Income taxes on the estate must be filed each year as long as there is continuing income to the estate. Once the estate is finally settled, this will cease. The only income that comes into the estate is usually in the form of dividends on investments previously held by the deceased. Other possible sources are:

- Proceeds from the sale of real estate held by the deceased
- Income tax return from the previous year's taxes
- Sale of vehicles or other possessions
- Proceeds from retirement accounts or 401(k)'s, etc.

G. Investment Accounts, Stocks, and Bonds

When these accounts exist, there will likely be a financial consultant assigned to the accounts. If so, contact this person for assistance with these matters. Decisions will have to be made about whether to transfer or redeem such accounts. Legal and financial advice from appropriate advisors is important in these matters.

H. Real Estate

Real estate to be sold should also be dealt with through appropriate contacts. If there is a home or other property to be sold, you must make some decisions about how to accomplish this—whether to list it yourself or to have a professional realtor involved. In that case, the realtor can advise you of the things that must be done. However, don't plan on a sale of a home right away. Allow sufficient time to clean out the home, and dispose of the household furniture and goods as discussed in this book. That can take some time to do correctly, so don't rush the sale of the home if it is possible to go at a slower pace.

I. Social Security Death Benefit

At the time of this writing, there is still a *Social Security Death Benefit* that will need to be claimed. Ask your attorney about how to go about doing this. Although it is not much, it is another item to which you are entitled.

11

When the Game Is Over: The Final Score

Although I never recall hearing the name of anyone whom my daddy assisted in the settlement of an estate, I do remember hearing stories around the dinner table about some of the nightmares people experienced while dealing with the final division process of an estate. Occasionally, my father's legal practice dealt with families involved in an estate settlement after a problem had developed. Many times these were initially caused by "little" things or even misunderstandings or minor situations, not major concerns or problems. Often the problems either involved spouses and children or family friends of the actual heirs. The cost of such problems always seemed to be far greater than they were worth. Certainly these things were not worth permanently damaging or scarring family relationships. I remember my father once commented that "people sometimes throw away their lifelong relationships for the silliest reasons."

As we began to face the task of settling our parents' estate, one thing stood out in all of our minds: *"Our Mother and Daddy would never forgive us if we let 'things' damage our relationships and cause problems among us."* We were immediately united in the decision to make this a peaceful and fair settlement and to remain friends for life. Therefore, what we now call *The Settlement Game* came about as a result of our comprehension of "what not to do" and of our putting to use the preventive methods suggested by our daddy as described in the preceding pages. Certain details of this process were added by us as we went through the actual stages of settling the estate.

Our parents had lived a love story. It became our responsibility to write the final chapter of their lives and to create some special and beautiful memories that represented them well. It was almost as if this was the final test of what they had taught us. It was up to us to prove that an estate could be settled in a fair and peaceful manner.

We did it! We are proud—of our parents, our heritage, ourselves, and the legacy that we can now pass on to our own children and heirs who will one day have to divide our estates. This book presents our method of settlement. We hope that whoever reads it will find it helpful in preventing damaged relationships within a family or perhaps in other associations. Life is too short to look back on it with regret.

It has now been several years since we settled our parents' estate. It was not extravagant, but they did have some lovely "things." Today, the four of us who are their

The love story of our parents, Eugene Albert Epting and Frances Thomas Epting. Married October 26, 1939, and celebrating their 50th wedding anniversary in 1989.

children and heirs are very good friends, and there are no grudges or feelings of resentment. We all feel a greater sense of family and closeness as a result of the process we went through. We each received a fair distribution of the furniture and other possessions in their home. Today these remind us of pleasant memories, not of strife and struggle to get them. We each received items we wanted and that reflect our individual personalities and lifestyles. We are all different, and through this method we each received the things that were most appropriate for us.

Take the time to do this right! We had so many good laughs over things we found. We discovered and shared pieces of history about our ancestors. We learned things about our parents' past that brought both smiles and tears. We shed tears over the loss of our parents, yet held dear the specialness of the two lives that had shaped our own being. We will always treasure the times we spent together settling the estate. It is a golden moment in time...treasure it—make it count—*it is forever!*

Appendix

There are several forms that will help you keep records during an estate settlement. In the pages that follow, samples of these are presented in a format suitable for copying. The design is intended to allow you to place the book on a copier so that you can make as many copies of each form as needed. Descriptions of each form follow:

1. **Appraisal List**—For use by an appraiser to list all items with monetary value to be divided by the heirs. It provides space for both descriptions and monetary values. (*Note:* Appraisers may have their own forms. Just be sure these forms present information in the way you need for it to appear for your purposes.)

2. **Interest Lists**—To be used by the heirs or participants for the purpose of listing items of particular interest to each. The format of this list provides space for the name and description of the item, as well as for the heir's specific reason for wanting or being entitled to the item.

3. **Distribution Sheets**—For use by heirs or participants to list their individual selections after they are chosen from each grouping. Both a description and the monetary value of the item should be listed.

4. **Tally Sheets**—For use in the final addition of total values for all selections for each heir. It is from this final form that the "baseline" is determined for the overall process. (See Chapter 7—Keeping Score.) It is from this form that the "Property Equalization" is accomplished. This is the main item that makes this process unique. Therefore, the Tally Sheets are the key to the peaceful and fair settlement of the estate. Be sure they are kept accurately.

5. **Household Accounts and Bills Record**—For use by the record keeper in listing and organizing all household accounts. This form can be used to record and track monthly household payments. The form can also be used to record dates when accounts are closed or finalized.

Appraisal List

This form is for use by an appraiser to list all items with monetary value to be divided by heirs. It provides space for descriptions along with respective values of items.

Note: If possible in your area, ask appraisers to quote you a "flat price" for this service as opposed to a percentage basis. Some appraisers who use the percentage method may value items higher because of the positive impact on their fee. If you can only find appraisers who use the percentage method, negotiate a "fee cap" at the very least. There are reputable services available for this. Ask for recommendations from a legal counsel, financial planners or others whom you trust. Especially ask appraiser candidates for references, and be sure to check them out. A good appraiser is worth a great deal in this process—so find one who is reputable and ethical.

To hire a professional appraiser, look for those listed in your area who are affiliated with either the American Society of Appraisers (ASA) or the Appraisers Association of America (AAA). These organizations have a code of ethics and abide by the Uniform Standards of Professional Appraisal Practice (USPAP) set forth by the Appraisal Foundation in Washington. To become a certified member of either of these organizations, candidates must prove their qualification through both evaluative efforts and examinations to show technical appraisal proficiency. Both associations have a membership directory. For online information, including how to find members in your region, go to one of the following websites:

American Society of Appraisers: www.appraisers.org

Appraisers Assoc. of America, Inc.: www.appraisersassoc.org

APPRAISAL LIST:

Appraiser's Name_____   Date_____

Category_____

Name of Item	General Description of Item	Monetary Value

Interest Lists

This form is to be used by the heirs or participants for the purpose of listing items of particular interest to each. The format provides space for the name and description of the item, as well as for a reason why the heir wants this item or feels entitled to it.

(From Chapter 4—The Game Setup) Before any dividing begins, have each of the participants make a list of any items they feel they have a claim to, or items of particular interest. For each item listed, give a brief explanation for why the item is wanted or why one feels it can be claimed. (Sometimes the reasons may be as simple as "because they had previously given the item as a gift.") This should be done privately, and the number of items of this sort should be limited to five each (ten at most). The heirs should then meet to decide about these items of special interest before going forward. If the item is uncontested and all can agree without a problem, then that heir gets the item requested. If any item begins to foster dispute or controversy, even in a friendly manner, or if one of the other heirs has also listed that item, it goes back into the general pool.)

INTEREST LIST:

Heir's Name _____ Date _____

1. Name and general description of item _____

Why have claim or reason wanted: _____

_____

_____

2. Name and general description of item _____

Why have claim or reason wanted: _____

_____

_____

3. Name and general description of item _____

Why have claim or reason wanted:

_____

_____

4. Name and general description of item _____

Why have claim or reason wanted:

_____

_____

5. Name and general description of item _____

Why have claim or reason wanted:

_____

_____

_____

Distribution Sheets

These are for use by heirs or participants in listing their individual selections after they are chosen from each grouping. Both the item description and the respective monetary value should be listed.

(From Chapter 4—The Game Setup). Make a sheet for each heir or participant. Each item selected should be listed in one column by name and description, with monetary value listed in an adjacent and corresponding column. (Use the list from the appraiser for this task.)

This listing process is essential to achieving an "equal" division of property. Be sure to recognize how important it is always to record each item with its corresponding monetary value assigned. Also, from our experience, we discovered that it is vital to record each item immediately when it is selected. No matter how good intentions are, it is easy to forget or to skip something if things are not done in this order.

DISTRIBUTION SHEET

Name of Heir or Participant_____   Date_____

Name of Item	General Description	Assigned Monetary Value

Tally Sheets

These are for use in the final addition of total values for all selections by each heir. It is from this final form that the "baseline" is determined for the overall process.

(From Chapter 6—Keeping Score) It is from this form that the "Property Equalization" is accomplished. This is the main item that makes this process unique. Therefore, the Tally Sheets are the key to the peaceful and fair settlement of the estate. Be sure they are kept accurately.

(From Chapter 7—Keeping Score) After all the groupings are complete and all selections made, it is important to tally the dollar value for each participant. Then the list with the highest monetary value can be used as the baseline for the others.

Before any money from the estate is divided in any other manner, it is used to balance out the lists so that each participant receives an equal compensation related to the material things and property in the estate.

For the sake of simplicity, the following form leaves room for up to four heirs or participants. If there are more, then of course a second copy of the form would be needed. Using the Distribution Sheets, enter the total dollar value in a column for each individual. If you have totaled items in categories or have subtotals, you may wish to make several entries and then add them up for a final total for each heir. After determining the highest value, indicate on the form the amount of money each of the other heirs should receive in order to equal that same amount. This equalization process brings the value of what all heirs are inheriting to the same level.

TALLY SHEET

1. Name_____

    Highest Value = BASE AMOUNT $ _____

    Total monetary value of selected items: —$ _____

            Amount due to Equalize Estate: $ _____

2. Name_____

    Highest Value = BASE AMOUNT $ _____

    Total monetary value of selected items: —$ _____

            Amount due to Equalize Estate: $ _____

3. Name_____

Highest Value = BASE AMOUNT $_____

Total monetary value of selected items: — $_____

Amount due to Equalize Estate: $_____

4. Name_____

Highest Value = BASE AMOUNT $_____

Total monetary value of selected items: — $_____

Amount due to Equalize Estate: $_____

Household Accounts and Bills Record

For use by the record keeper in listing and organizing all household accounts. This form can be used to track and record monthly household payments. It can also be used to record dates when accounts are closed or finalized.

(From Chapter 10—Final Stats: The "To-Do" List) If the account can be canceled, be sure to send notice to do so. Things such as credit cards, magazine subscriptions, memberships, or anything that does not need to be continued for the operation of the household should be canceled. (*Note: Do not* just destroy credit cards—you must cancel them officially. Be sure to keep records of these notifications as proof of the cancellation.)

Household accounts that are needed for a home to continue functioning must be continued. These might include such things as telephone, water, electricity, gas, home insurance, and miscellaneous household accounts. If there is a vehicle that will continue to be used, be sure to continue car insurance until such vehicle is transferred or sold.

HOUSEHOLD ACCOUNTS AND BILLS RECORD

For Month of _____

As bills come in, log information below and attach statement to back of this form.

Keep together monthly. Attach any proof of action on accounts.

NOTE: When account is paid in full and closed, write CLOSED in Balance Due Column and attach documentation.

Due Date	Name of Account or Bill	Amount	Amt. Paid	Bal. Due

U.S. Supreme Court

McDANIEL v. BARRESI, 402 U.S. 39 (1971)

402 U.S. 39

McDANIEL, SUPERINTENDENT OF SCHOOLS, ET AL. v. BARRESI ET AL.
CERTIORARI TO THE SUPREME COURT OF GEORGIA
No. 420.
Argued October 13, 1970
Decided April 20, 1971

The Board of Education of Clarke County, Ga. (with a two-to-one white-Negro elementary school system ratio), devised a student assignment plan for desegregating elementary schools which establishes geographic zones drawn to promote desegregation and also provides that pupils in heavily concentrated Negro "pockets" walk or go by bus to schools in other attendance zones. The resulting Negro elementary enrollment ranges from 20% to 40% in all but two schools, where it is 50%. Respondent parents sued to enjoin the plan's operation. The state trial court denied an injunction. The Georgia Supreme Court reversed, holding that the plan violated (1) equal protection because it "[treated] students differently because of their race," and (2) the Civil Rights Act of 1964, because Title IV prohibits a school board from requiring busing to achieve a racial balance. Held:

1. In compliance with its duty to convert to a unitary system, the school board properly took race into account in fixing the attendance lines. P. 41.

2. Title IV, a direction to federal officials, does not restrict state officials in assigning students within their systems. Pp. 41-42.

226 Ga. 456, 175 S. E. 2d 649, reversed.

BURGER, C. J., delivered the opinion for a unanimous Court.

Eugene A. Epting argued the cause and filed a brief for petitioners.

E. Freeman Leverett argued the cause and filed a brief for respondents.

Briefs of amici curiae were filed by Solicitor General Griswold and Assistant Attorney General Leonard for the United States, and by Arthur K. Bolton, Attorney General, Harold N. Hill, Jr., Executive Assistant Attorney General, and Alfred L. Evans, Jr., and J. Lee Perry, Assistant Attorneys General, for the State of Georgia. [402 U.S. 39, 40]

MR. CHIEF JUSTICE BURGER delivered the opinion of the Court.

We granted certiorari in this case to review a state court order enjoining the operation of a school desegregation plan. The action was brought in the Superior Court of Clarke County, Georgia, by parents of children attending public elementary schools in that county. Named as defendants were the Superintendent of Education and members of the Clarke County Board of Education. The trial court denied respondents' request for an injunction, but on appeal the Supreme Court of Georgia reversed, 226 Ga. 456, 175 S. E. 2d 649 (1970). This Court then granted certiorari, 400 U.S. 804 (1970).

Beginning in 1963, the Clarke County Board of Education began a voluntary program to desegregate its public schools. The student-assignment plan presently at issue, involving only elementary schools, has been in effect since the start of the 1969 academic year. The plan, adopted by the Board of Education and approved by the Department of Health, Education, and Welfare,[1] relies primarily upon geographic attendance zones drawn to achieve greater racial balance. Additionally, the pupils in five heavily Negro "pockets" either walk or are transported by bus to schools located in other attendance zones.[2] As a consequence the Negro enrollment of each [402 U.S. 39, 41] elementary school in the system varies generally between 20% and 40%, although two schools have a 50% Negro enrollment. The white-Negro ratio of elementary pupils in the system is approximately two to one.

Respondents contend in this action that the board's desegregation plan violates the Fourteenth Amendment of the Federal Constitution and Title IV of the Civil Rights Act of 1964. The Supreme Court of Georgia upheld both contentions, concluding first that the plan violated the Equal Protection Clause "by treating students differently because of their race." The court concluded also that Title IV prohibited the board from "requiring the transportation of pupils or students from one school to another...in order to achieve such racial balance..." We reject these contentions.

The Clarke County Board of Education, as part of its affirmative duty to disestablish the dual school system, properly took into account the race of its elementary school children in drawing attendance lines. To have done otherwise would have severely hampered the board's ability to deal effectively with the task at hand. School boards that operated dual school systems are "clearly charged with the affirmative duty to take whatever steps might be necessary to convert to a unitary system in which racial discrimination would be eliminated root and branch." Green v. County School Board, 391 U.S. 430, 437 -438 (1968). In this remedial process, steps will almost invariably require that students be assigned "differently because of their race." See Swann

v. Charlotte-Mecklenburg Board of Education, ante, p. 1; Young-blood v. Board of Public Instruction, 430 F.2d 625, 630 (CA5 1970). Any other approach would freeze the status quo that is the very target of all desegregation processes.

Nor is the board's plan barred by Title IV of the Civil Rights Act of 1964. The sections relied upon by respondents (42 U.S.C. 2000c (b), 2000c-6) are directed [402 U.S. 39, 42] only at federal officials and are designed simply to foreclose any interpretation of the Act as expanding the powers of federal officials to enforce the Equal Protection Clause. Swann, supra, at 17. Title IV clearly does not restrict state school authorities in the exercise of their discretionary powers to assign students within their school systems.

Reversed.

Footnotes

1. It may well be that the Board of Education adopted the present student-assignment plan because of urgings of federal officials and fear of losing federal financial assistance. The state trial court, however, made no findings on these matters. No federal officials are parties in this case.

2. Where the distance between the student's residence and his assigned school is more than 1½ miles, free transportation is provided. There is no challenge here to the feasibility of the transportation provisions of the plan. The annual transportation expenses of the present plan are reported in the record to be $11,070 less than the school system spent on transportation during the 1968-1969 school year under dual operation. [402 U.S. 39, 43]

Griffin Bell Biography

Griffin B. Bell is a senior counsel in the law firm of King and Spalding, LLP.

Judge Bell was born in Americus, Georgia, on 31 October 1918. From 1941 to 1946, he served in the U.S. Army, attaining the rank of major. In 1948, he graduated *cum laude* from Mercer University Law School in Macon with an LL.B. degree. He has received the Order of the Coif from Vanderbilt Law School and honorary degrees from Mercer University and several other colleges and universities.

From 1948 to 1961, he practiced law in Georgia, joining King & Spalding in 1953 and becoming its managing partner in 1958. He served as senior partner until 1 January 2004, at which time he became senior counsel for the firm.

Judge Bell was appointed by President John F. Kennedy to the U.S. Court of Appeals for the Fifth Circuit in 1961. Judge Bell served on the Fifth Circuit for 15 years until 1976 and during that time was a director of the Federal Judicial Center. In December 1976, President Jimmy E. Carter nominated him to become the 72nd Attorney General of the United States. Judge Bell received the oath of office from Chief Justice Warren E. Burger in January 1977 and served as Attorney General until August 1979.

During 1980, Judge Bell led the American delegation to the Conference on Security and Cooperation in Europe, held in Madrid. In 1981, he served as Co-Chairman of the Attorney General's National Task Force on Violent Crime. He received the Thomas Jefferson Memorial Foundation Award in 1984 for excellence in law.

In 1985–86, Judge Bell served as President of the American College of Trial Lawyers. From 1985 to 1987, he served on the Secretary of State's Advisory Committee on South Africa. He also was a Director of the Ethics Resource Center for several years and in 1986 served as its Chairman of the Board. From 1986 to 1989, Judge Bell served as a member of the Board of Trustees of the Foundation for the Commemoration of the United States Constitution. In 1989, he accepted an appointment as Vice Chairman of President George H. W. Bush's Commission on Federal Ethics Law Reform. During the Independent Counsel's investigation of the Iran-Contra Affair, Judge Bell represented President Bush.

Judge Bell continues to practice law and is active in issues involving the U.S. Constitution and our nation's judicial system. In 2002, Judge Bell served on Secretary Rumsfeld's ad hoc Advisory Committee on new rules governing military tribunals. He also served on the Webster Commission, which in March 2002 issued its report on FBI security programs and Russian spy Robert Hanssen. In 2003, he served on the Technology and Privacy Advisory Committee for the Department of Defense and chaired a study group regarding the FBI's Office of Professional Responsibility. Recently, he was selected by the Department of Defense to be a member of the Review Panel for Military Commissions, an appointment that carries the rank of Major General.

About the Author

Angie Epting Morris

Angie Epting Morris is the daughter of attorney Eugene A. Epting of Athens, Georgia. From her years growing up, she remembers her father's stories about estate settlements and his advice on how to avoid family conflict in these situations. When both of her parents died in 1993, she—along with her two sisters and her brother—faced the task of settling the estate. By putting to use the advice of their father, they were able to accomplish this with remarkable success. They emerged from the process as better friends than they had been when they started and remain close still.

After ten years of giving out this information to many friends and acquaintances, and after receiving back countless stories of praise and gratitude for the enlightening advice, Angie began realizing she should take this message to the world. When her husband's mother passed away in 2003, he asked Angie to give copies of this information to his brothers and sister so they could use it to settle her estate. After this "vote of confidence" from those who knew her best, she concluded this was indeed something that would help many people facing similar circumstances in years to come. It is her hope that it will assist others in achieving peaceful estate settlements, thereby protecting family relationships and helping families avoid conflict.

Angie graduated from the University of Georgia in 1968 with a B.S. degree in geography and majored in cartography (i.e., map making). This led to employment as a professional cartographer for the Department of Agriculture in Washington, D.C., in 1969. There she had a blind date with Carter Morris, a young Naval Officer who was serving as a White House military social aide. After they were married in 1972, they made their home in Evans, Georgia, outside of Augusta, and raised two sons, Hunter and Taylor, now grown. Carter became a high school teacher and coach. Angie taught high school English and geography for three years before opening a retail travel agency in Augusta. She also eventually opened a state accredited travel school to train travel industry personnel, which she operated simultaneously with the agency. These experiences added to her qualifications as a teacher—only now she instructs others on the process of estate settlement. She has become recognized as an expert on "How to Settle an Estate Peacefully and Fairly." Not only does she tell you what to do, but she also gives specific instructions on how to do this with a step-by-step guide called *The Settlement Game: How to Settle an Estate Peacefully and Fairly.*

The Settlement Game Organization Kit

With attractive and convenient canvas duck tote.

The Settlement Game Organization Kit will provide you with everything you need to organize the estate settlement.

- The book, ***The Settlement Game: How to Settle an Estate Peacefully and Fairly***
- 3-ring binder with dividers to assist with separate record-keeping functions
- All forms required for the process
- Color-coded tags and stickers for labeling selections
- Miscellaneous office supplies: petty cash bag; receipt book, calculator, dice, and more
- The book, ***Positive Personality Profiles***, by Dr. Robert A. Rohm
- A stylish embroidered tote bag made of duck canvas cotton twill. It will accommodate all of The Settlement Game Organization Kit Supplies, and provides a convenient way to transport documents and supplies needed to complete the estate settlement process.

The Settlement Game Organization Kit sells for $69.00 plus tax (if applicable) and shipping. Either order online at www.thesettlement game.com or use the order form on the next page.

Give the Gift of
The Settlement Game
How to Settle an Estate Peacefully and Fairly
to Your Friends and Colleagues

CHECK YOUR LEADING BOOKSTORE OR ORDER HERE

❑ **YES,** I want _____ copies of *The Settlement Game* at $14.95 each (Ohio residents please add $1.08 sales tax plus $4.95 shipping per book. Georgia residents please add $1.05 sales tax plus $4.95 shipping per book.) Canadian orders must be accompanied by a postal money order in U.S. funds. Allow 15 days for delivery.

❑ **YES,** I want _____ copies of *Positive Personality Profiles* by Dr. Robert A. Rohm at $12.95 each.

❑ **YES,** I want _____ sets of *The Settlement Game Organization Kit* at $69.00 each.

My check or money order for $_____ is enclosed.

Please charge my: ❑ Visa   ❑ MasterCard
                  ❑ Discover ❑ American Express

Name _____

Organization _____

Address _____

City/State/Zip _____

Phone_____ Email _____

Card # _____

Exp. Date_____ Signature _____

Order online at **www.thesettlementgame.com**

OR *Please make your check payable and return to:*
BookMasters, Inc. • 30 Amberwood Parkway • Ashland, OH 44805
Call your credit card order to (800) 247-6553
Fax (419) 281-6883